More praise for
WANDERING GIRL

"Honest and unaffected . . .
Worthwhile."
School Library Journal

"An authentic, honest account of
injustice."
The Kirkus Reviews

DISCARDED

WANDERING GIRL

Glenyse Ward

FAWCETT JUNIPER • NEW YORK

RLI: $\dfrac{\text{VL: 5 \& up}}{\text{IL: 6 \& up}}$

A Fawcett Juniper Book
Published by Ballantine Books
Text Copyright © 1988 by Glenyse Ward

Library of Congress Catalog Card Number: 90-48825

ISBN 0-449-70414-9

This edition published by arrangement with Henry Holt & Company.

Manufactured in the United States of America

First Ballantine Books Edition: June 1992

*For my mother, husband, and children,
and for all the Aboriginal women who,
as girls, had to face hard times working on
white people's farms in the Great Southern
and other districts of their own country.*

Contents

I would like to acknowledge the generous assistance of the Aboriginal Arts Board in providing funds to develop this book. Thanks to Jack Davis and Colin Johnson for the inspiration they have given me and the editorial help; also to the staff of Magabala Books for their time and effort. Finally and most importantly, thanks to my family for having the faith to urge me on.   G.W.

From the Author

My name is Glenyse Ward (maiden name, Spratt). I was born in 1949 in Perth, Western Australia. I was taken away from my natural parents at the age of one, because Mum took me to see a doctor when I was sick. The Native Welfare was called in, and Mum was told she was an unfit mother and I would be better off put into a home and reared up the European way.

You see, in the early days of survival and struggle, there was a lot of hardship and agony amongst the Aboriginal people. Through the misguided minds of earnest white people we were taken away from our natural parents. This affected all of us. Put into missions, forced to abide by the European way, we lost our identity.

I was put into an orphanage called St. John of God, run by the order of St. John of God's nuns. It was situated in a suburb of Perth called Rivervale. From there I was picked by a Catholic priest and brother, Father Leuman and Brother Lenard, who were of German descent, and driven down in an old grey ute to a mission, St. Francis Xavier Native Mission, Wandering Brook, which was eighty miles south of Perth. It was there that I did my schooling and grew up. I wasn't a bright student, I never made the grades to attend a school in Perth, and so I was made a working girl at the mission. That meant you had to help the nuns with domestic chores. So I ended up washing pots and pans until I was old enough, like fifteen or sixteen, to take on an outside job—which meant working for upper-class white people, washing their pots and pans.

After a year of madness I broke away to hang on to what bit of sanity I had left, and found my own independency working as a domestic in the kitchen at Busselton Hospital. From there I went to Perth and became involved in different fields of work, like nursing assistant in a couple of big hospitals in Perth. I then joined Community Health Services and worked with them for about six to seven years. It was during that time, around the seventies, I met my husband, Charles, a qualified hairdresser. We were married in 1975 and have two children, a boy, Brian Ocean, and a girl, Jodi Anne. We now reside in Broome in the north of Western Australia. Charles has taken a different field of work. He is a full-time cook at the alcoholic rehabilitation centre in Broome. Our children attend the state school.

Since I finished this book, *Wandering Girl*, I am continuing to write. At the moment I am concentrating on writing a book about the mission, and hope to have that finished soon. I hope to get more knowledge on writing and publishing books, so one day I will be able to help my people.

The Mission

I was a baby when I was put into an orphanage called Saint Joseph's in Rivervale, run by the order of St. John of God. When I became the age of three, I was put into another home, which we called Wandering Mission. It was here that I spent the next thirteen years of my life.

The mission itself was very rich in nature; the whole surroundings were photogenic, set in a valley. We as little girls used to be very frightened of going near the hills to pick berries, as there were big caves up there.

The older girls would tell us there were devilmen living in those caves. *Mumaries*, they called them, and they were all hairy and ugly and used to come out at night. If we were naughty, they would come with a sack and get us, and put us in it and cart us away.

I just could not laugh today, thinking of how those big girls used to jump on my bed at night because my dormitory window had the best view of the hills. They used to tell us they could see lights flickering up there. The little hairy men were getting ready to come down! I put up with the pain of being half squashed because I felt safe with them all on top of me. Then one of the older girls would sing out, "Baalay—look out, they're coming!" And there would be screams, kids crying in a mad dash to their beds. I'd be running with them and jump into my mate's bed, still crying.

The mission was run by the Catholic Church. The nuns, priests, and brothers who were in charge of us were all of German descent. I remember when I first set eyes on the brothers. They seemed strange to me. We used to be frightened of them. They were very serious people, hardly ever smiling. They wore these things on their eyes, which looked so funny. And they wore big baggy pants, long-sleeved white shirts, and bits of string over their shoulders to hold up the baggy pants—braces!

The nuns wore about three or four dresses on them and all this cloth over their heads. When they walked towards us, we would run away and cry. They all spoke in a strange manner, which was a broken kind of English. When we were naughty, those nuns used to punish us, and instead of saying that we would get no sweets at night, they'd say, "You become no sweets tonight!" It took us a long time to get used to their language. In the end we used to run away laughing at it.

Our upbringing throughout our childhood years was very strict. Everyday activities were done to the ring of a bell and with prayers. The main principle was boys and girls had to be kept apart.

We slept in separate dormitories: boys up one end of the mission, girls down the other end. That went for everything else, too—church and school and dining room—boys up one end, girls down the other! When we were allowed out to play in the fields, the boys had their ground and we had ours. We even had our own dams to swim in, and if you got caught talking to boys or were found where you were not allowed to be, you would get a severe punishment or a belting.

Severe punishment would be: locked in a dark room at night with only a lantern to see by. You were made to darn socks up till one or two in the morning. We used to end up nervous wrecks after that!

Our clothes were all made of khaki material, with rick-rack braid all around the hems. Our bloomers were made of Dingo brand self-raising flour bags. If there had been a prize going for fashion in those days, I am sure we would have taken first.

Confession was every Saturday, and everybody had to go. Sometimes I couldn't understand why—we had nothing to confess to! If only I had known in those days what I know today. I would have had something to confess.

Although the mission was run very strict, we had our good times and our bad. From the age of six upwards, we each had our duties. We had to help in the dairy with farm chores. The brothers used to look after that part of things and we had to help—milking, collecting eggs, feeding the pigs, going out with the brothers to feed the cattle, checking windmills and so on.

I used to hate feeding the pigs. They terrified me, though I didn't mind the little piglets, as we used to chase them to see how many we could catch. Nor did I mind milking the cows, but for their business. My job was to shovel it up. The other kids used to tease me about this.

The brothers handled the machine that separated the milk and cream, but when they weren't around for a few moments, we'd have a good feed of cream. Our job was also to lock the young calves in a yard while their mothers were being milked. We would climb on their backs and ride them around.

Whenever we got up to mischief, we set a smaller girl as our lookout to see if any nuns or brothers were coming. Soon as she sang out, "They're coming!" we'd be all busy doing our work. Only sometimes the lookout girl might have a grudge against one of us and not give the warning.

Every month we had to change our duties, like whoever used to wash pots or wash the dishes, or clean the dining room up after meals, would change to the laundry duties or the kitchen duties, and or, and or . . .

We used to attend school at the mission. I guess I wasn't very bright, I stayed in grade seven for two years. I couldn't even tell the time when I left school to become a working girl on the mission. This meant you had to help on the mission till you were old enough, like fifteen or sixteen, to go out and work for white people.

The way I learnt to tell the time was through the nun I used to work with in the kitchen pointing at the different times she wanted me there to help her. If I wasn't there on time, I used to get a hit!

I'll never forget the Christmas parties we used to have at the mission every year. It was a sad time—sad because most of the kids used to go home to their families, while others like me always stayed behind. We had no one to go to. Instead we used to have to help do all the jobs, like the harvesting, though that used to be a lot of fun.

Out we would go into the paddocks with the brothers and some of the nuns. Since there weren't so many of us, we had a lot of privileges during the holidays. While we helped with the harvesting, we were allowed to take our dinners with us—sandwiches and cordial—and we were allowed to have as much cordial as we liked. Then we'd bog into our watermelon. One of the nuns would tell us we could go for a swim in the dam, which was nearby, and we'd scramble like chooks off to the water.

By the time the nun reached us, we'd be looking like drenched ducks in our dresses, as we never had bathers in those days. The nun used to sit on the bank of the dam, while the cattle were all around us, doing their business in the water. We'd be calling out to Sister to look at us diving and splashing.

When she thought we'd had enough swimming, she called out to us, but we used to make out we never heard her, and kept disappearing by ducking our heads under the brown surface. When we'd come up for fresh air, we'd look at Sister, and we could see from her face if we'd gone too far.

So we'd race one another back to our work until in the evening we'd go with all the nuns for a walk about two miles down the road. One of the nuns would chuck lollies out to us from her apron pockets, and we all scrambled over the ground to get our fair share. Then every Sunday we would be off to the nearest town for a picnic, and the brothers or nuns used to buy us each an ice cream, which we did look forward to. We used to lick it slow, so as to make it last longer, although it would melt on us and make us lick faster than we wanted to.

The Christmas party brought us all together like one happy family. This was the only time I felt close to everyone, because all year around we did things separately.

The brothers would go out and cut down a big pine tree, then bring it back and plant it in a large bin of sand. Us girls used to help the nuns decorate the tree and dining room. Come nighttime the whole dining room would be lit up with candles and coloured lights. All the priests and brothers and nuns used to be there. Then one of the nuns would start to play the organ to the tune of "Silent Night." We joined in with them, though they sang in German. We learnt a lot of the German language in the mission!

When the carols were finished, we would make a dash to the table to find our presents. The nuns were like real mums. I reckon the look on our little faces, when we opened up our presents and cuddled our peg dolls, brought a tear to their eyes. I suppose they were missing their families in Germany too.

After all the festivities were over, everything got back to normal. And so the years went by until one particular spring morning when I awoke feeling very emotional. For the first time in my life I was leaving my home, at the age of sixteen years. I didn't know what to expect. I was frightened. I didn't want to go—but I had no choice.

There was no time for tears or good-byes. The nuns had all my clothes packed. Everything was brand-new. "Oh, God," I thought. "I am going to miss these dear nuns."

I said good-bye to all my mates in a very emotional state. Then the white people arrived to take me away. They were in a smart car, and both were well dressed, old looking, about fifty I suppose. The man was short and round, with a plump face and beady eyes. His wife was short too but slim, with a lined face and turned-up nose. She had a dainty look.

The father in charge introduced me to them, and told me I had to work for these nice people.

And not to forget to say my prayers, as he would be ringing up from time to time to find out how I was progressing in my work. Then he gave me a pat on the back, and the lady opened the back door of the car. I got in and sat down nervously.

As the car sped on my journey into the unknown, I sat back with a feeling of anguish and grief. The journey was quiet for most of the way, the man and woman just making conversation between themselves, and I dozed off to sleep.

Dark Servant

When I awoke, we were driving through this pretty town. The lady turned to me and told me we were nearing our destination. Just a couple of miles beyond the town and we would be there, at their farm.

The countryside was very picturesque. There were big hills all around, which reminded me of my Wandering home. We drove on for another mile, and the man slowed down. He veered off to the right. I looked up as he stopped the car to get out and open the gate. It was getting on dusk, and I saw lights on the hill. It looked real pretty from down here.

We bounced over this bridge with a little brook running under it. The ducks seemed so content, just paddling with the flow of the water.

We drove up to the house, and in the driveway he stopped the car. The house looked enormous! The woman turned to me and told me to get out. She climbed out herself and told me to follow her inside, which I did.

We went into the kitchen and sat down. She

said she'd put the kettle on and make a cup of
tea and that she shouldn't be long, as she was
going to her room to freshen up after the long
journey.

I sat there feeling rather uneasy and on edge,
got up, and thought I'd take a peep into the next
room. What I saw took my breath away!

The floor was covered in a beautiful, dark,
rich, red carpet. The furniture was all antique
and shone magnificently. The silverware, placed
effectively around the room, glittered viva-
ciously. Even the brickwork around the open
fireplace was polished up to a deep, dark, red
colour, and the chandelier hanging from the
ceiling sparkled like a jewel.

In one way I was glad I had come to this nice
place. I couldn't wait to write back to the mission to tell my mates. Then I heard footsteps
coming, so I quickly went to sit on my chair—
innocently!

They came in, and the man sat down while
she pottered around getting the tea things ready.
I sat very quietly there, listening to their conversation, which they were having between
themselves.

When everything was ready, she sat down,
turned to me, and told me their names were
Mr. and Mrs. Bigelow.

As she poured herself and Mr. Bigelow tea
in beautiful cups and saucers, I wondered if I
was going to get a cup. I could only see two
cups and saucers on the table when she went to
a cupboard in the far left of the kitchen and I

thought, "Oh, that's good; she's going to get me a cup and saucer." To my amazement she came back to the table with an old tin mug, poured tea in it, and placed it down in front of me.

She must have seen the bewilderment on my face as I looked at her. I wasn't the type of person to speak out, being brought up in a strict environment. We were taught never to speak out to people unless we were spoken to first, no matter what the circumstances.

I politely asked her if I could have a cup and saucer to drink from, as I wasn't used to drinking out of tin mugs and never had done so in the mission.

The answer I received back was in a very irate and furious tone of voice. She stated to me that I was there as her dark servant, that I was to obey her orders and do what she told me to do! I took the tin mug and drank my tea with a very confused mind.

Now that we had our cup of tea, Mr. Bigelow said he was retiring to the lounge. Mrs. Bigelow said she'd take me to my room—which I couldn't wait to see, as I imagined it to be like the beautiful dining room I'd seen.

So we went out the back door of the kitchen, away from that nice room, up some stairs, and past an old shower room. It looked like a place where she'd keep her dogs. I had caught a glimpse of them as I came in.

We passed a big rack of shoes, went up another set of steps, then she opened a door and switched on the lights. I wondered where my nice room was: We were in a garage!

She opened a door on her left, reached up, and got an old burner down from a hook—and lit it.

Through the dim light of the lantern I saw my case standing next to the old wooden bed. I cried out, and asked her what my case was doing in this horrible dirty room. Could she have possibly made a mistake?

I suppose I shouldn't have asked, as I only burdened myself more by having to be told sharply, I was her dark servant! This room was to be my bedroom while I was here working for her.

She continued on with a fierce tirade of orders, saying she wanted me to be up bright and early. If I looked in the cupboard next to the bed I would find an old alarm clock. I was to set it to five o'clock. Just outside my door, in the garage, I would find a big straw broom. With that broom I was to sweep her driveway, which, as I later found, went for about a mile around her house and finished down near some gates leading to the orchard. After that I was to go and wait for her in the kitchen to get my orders for the rest of the day.

With a haughty look about herself, she strutted out the door, leaving me with feelings of animosity and humiliation. I fumbled through my case to find my nightdress and slowly put it on, blew the flame out, and got that old familiar feeling called homesickness. I cried myself to sleep.

Orange Juice in the Morning

When I awoke, it was to the shrill sound of the alarm clock. I reached over and turned it off, then lay back on my pillow to familiarize with my new surroundings. When I recalled where I was, my heart sank. I jolted out of bed and thought I'd make a good impression on my first day, though I had no heart for it at all.

I lit the old burner up to see what I was doing. I got my working clothes out of my case, a clean set of underwear, a dress which came down to the ankles, a full-length apron, shoes, ankle socks, and a scarf so the wind wouldn't blow my hair around while I was sweeping the driveway.

It was still pretty dark when I opened up my bedroom door. The wind was blowing and howling, and the light from the lamp was reflecting on every obstacle, making the whole surroundings pretty scary.

I hesitated, stepped back inside the room, and thought to myself, "I'll have a wash later on when I finish sweeping, as it will be lighter and I can see a bit better."

So I got dressed and tried hard not to be frightened. When I was ready, I picked up the old burner, set all my fears aside, got the old straw broom, and started sweeping.

I put the lantern in between two bushes so the wind wouldn't blow it out, and with big strokes I began to sweep her driveway. What a job that was! The more I swept the leaves, the more the wind would blow them back on the path.

When I finished the job, I was ready for that wash, all hot and frustrated! By this time it was real light, so I checked again to see if the driveway was clean, put the broom back in the garage, and went to my room to hang the old burner up on the hook, then got my toiletries out to have myself a wash.

The shower room matched up with my bedroom, dull and listless with a terrible dog smell about it. I walked around a bit and came across what I assumed was the laundry. I shut the two doors, and had a wash in one of the big old basins.

When I finished I chucked Johnson's baby powder all over me so I could smell nice, cleaned up the mess I had made, then went around the laundry to use the toilet, which was in the same block. Now that I was all clean, I made my way into the kitchen to wait for Mrs. Bigelow to give me my orders for the day.

Everything was quiet when I went in and sat down at the table. Then I heard someone moving around in the next room. So thinking it was her, I thought I'd better go in, say good morning, and let her know I was there.

I poked my head around the door and saw Mr. Bigelow sitting there having a cup of coffee and reading the paper. I said, ''Good morning, sir!''

He never lifted an eyelid. He just told me to go and wait in the kitchen for Mrs. Bigelow. I felt ashamed and embarrassed as I went back into the kitchen to sit down.

I heard her coming. She had a pompous, stately look about her, which made me feel timid and afraid. She asked me if I had completed sweeping the driveway. I said yes; then she turned to me to tell me about another job she would like me to do.

Before breakfast I was to go down a fair way from the house where her orchard grew. On one side of it was a paddock, in which one orange tree stood alone behind a high fence. I was to go over and pick two oranges, run back to the house, squeeze the juice into a clean glass, and put a starched doyley over it, as when she got up in the mornings she must have fresh orange juice.

I asked her if she wanted me to go and do the job at once. She said yes, so off I went to tackle it.

On my way down to the paddock, I stopped to view the countryside. Very pretty, the gullies and the sweeping plains. The big hills that surrounded the property brought memories to me of my home!

When I got to the big fence, I wondered how I was going to climb over it without ripping my clothing. I tucked my dress in my bloomers, chucked my shoes off, and with shaky, wobbly vibrations climbed over the fence, ran to the tree, and picked two oranges off. Then it was back over, shoes on, and back to the house to get her juice ready for her.

She was already sitting at the breakfast table in the dining room, so I bolded in bravely and put the orange juice in front of her—only to be scolded, and reminded in a harsh manner that I wasn't allowed in the dining room while any member of the family was there unless she rang the bell; then I had to go in and see to her needs.

I begged her pardon, and asked if I might have my breakfast.

She told me I was to use my tin plate and mug. I could help myself to weeties, have one piece of bread and butter and a cup of tea—bacon and eggs were out for her dark slave.

So I thanked her and went into the kitchen to satisfy my appetite. I piled my tin plate high with weeties, because in the mission weeties were like a luxury to us kids.

We only had them once a week. That was every Sunday after church. If we never sang our songs or said our prayers during church, our punishment was that we got no weeties! The nuns used to stand in line behind us in the pews and check to see who was singing. So we sang till our lungs just about burst, as we knew we could look forward to a nice bowl of weeties. Although they were put into a big pot of boiling water and used to go all mushy, they were still weeties and a far cry from old starchy porridge and mouldy bread with buttermilk. If the kids at the mission could see me now helping myself to the weeties, fresh milk, and plenty of sugar, how envious they would be.

I wasn't quite sure how much weeties I could have. I just helped myself, and ate quickly before she came in to tell me that I had enough! After I finished eating, I sat back feeling rather bloated. The bell rang. I jumped up and went in to see what she wanted.

She was wiping away the traces of her breakfast from around her mouth in a rather disdainful manner. She put down her serviette to tell me that she was writing down a list of duties for me, and that she expected the jobs to be done properly. In the meantime I was to go into the kitchen and tidy it up and wait till she was ready for me with her list.

So I walked back into the kitchen to tidy up. I was beginning to feel like a zombie, beginning to feel that my sanity was slipping. To hang on to it, I thought I'd sing a few songs and get rid of those remorseful feelings I had churning up inside of me. So I started to sing one of my favourite songs, learnt at the mission: "I love to go a'wandering along the mountain track . . ."

I had really engrossed myself and my thoughts into my song, when I was startled and interrupted rudely and told to stop that dreadful noise.

I must have really upset her this time as her face was red as a beetroot. She told me she was very cross with me, as I was here as her servant, and she wasn't allowing her servants to go around making noises. She stated I was here to work for her, and if I wasn't going to listen to her, I would be reported to the mission. Then she asked me, ''Do you understand me clearly?''

I said, ''Yes, Mrs. Bigelow,'' but deep down inside, I couldn't understand her and her attitude towards me. I thought she was quite a strange person. I didn't dare say anything or speak out, for fear of being scolded; I had to just grin and bear it.

You see, in those days I thought that's how people treated you. I didn't know any other way of life. This was the first place I had come to fresh out of the mission, so I was starting to feel a little bit resentful towards her.

I continued on with my work. When she came in and handed me my list of jobs, I nearly buckled at the knees. I felt very weak at the thought of all that work. She just told me to pull myself together and follow her, as she would show me around the house and where to find the cleaning things.

I felt frightened, as I didn't know how I'd keep my energy or strength of mind up; frightened, for fear I might not finish in the time she wanted me to, and I would end up getting a scolding.

While I followed on beside her, she was pointing out particular jobs that needed doing. I couldn't quite focus my mind or pay attention to her. My mind was far away, thinking of home and how the other kids were getting on. I wouldn't feel so bad if some of them were here with me; I'd feel real happy. But I knew that was not to be.

When she left me standing there with the list in my hands, my mind came back to reality. I started on my first duty, which was to gather all the silver and brassware, and polish and shine it until I could see my face in it. Then I had to go around and wax and polish all the woodwork—from windows to skirting boards. Even the bricks around the fireplace had to be polished! Then I had to wash and sponge the carpet down. Then all the windows had to be cleaned. After all that was done, on to the next room and go through the same routine.

I had to put every effort into making this room spotless. It was the room where she entertained all the Very Important People. Mr. Bigelow was Lord Mayor of the town and surrounding districts.

People used to come from everywhere—not that it mattered to me. I was only there to clean and sweep up.

Whenever they were entertaining or having a party at night, I was never allowed to be seen. I had to go straight to bed. My orders were, I was not allowed anywhere near the house. It was out of bounds to her dark servant, because she didn't want the embarrassment of me amongst her supercilious friends. The sight of me might have put their toffee noses out of joint!

I shall never forget one of those lavish parties she threw. All the High Society was there. I remember the preparation I had to put into it—forever cleaning, mopping, shining things up for days. Her daughter came from town to help her mother. I couldn't see any sense in why she came, since I had to do everything.

As well as my cleaning jobs, I had to do all the kitchen duties, like preparing the veggies, washing the pots, pans, cleaning the walls etc., etc. . . . Making sure the pantry was spotless, washing and waxing the lino of the kitchen floor—all her daughter did was stir the pots of food on the stove.

I heard her say to her daughter that this party was something to do with elections. I didn't understand what that meant; I just carried on with my work, getting things ready so everything would look nice for her party.

Now on the night, she came to me all done up in a long lime-green evening gown. Her daughter was there too, dressed in a silvery-white gown. Like her mother, she was dainty, with a turned-up nose and plenty of rouge and lipstick on. A real "pretty kid," as we say.

Their necklaces and earrings were of beautiful pale-blue colours, but with all that makeup and rouge on, they both looked like clowns. As

I'd never seen women dressed up like that, it was something new to me—I thought they looked quite comical!

Anyway, she came over to give me strict instructions. When all her guests arrived, I was to take her two grandchildren into the back room—what she used to call the sleepout. I was to look after her grand-kids in that room. I wasn't allowed to show myself to her guests, so she left me and the kids there while she went to greet them.

I settled the kids down. When they fell asleep, I looked out the door—cars were everywhere. I took a look at the kids; they were sound asleep. So I thought I'd better go and help Mrs. Bigelow, me feeling sorry for her and thinking she might need a hand with all those people. So kindhearted me bolded into the V.I.P. room, looking like a real Orphan Annie.

Soon as I opened the door, all the chatter and laughter stopped. You could hear a pin drop, as all eyes were on me. All of a sudden, some poshed-up voice, with a plum in her mouth, came out of the crowd. "Tracey, dear, is this your little dark servant?"

I just stood there smiling. I thought it was wonderful that at last people were taking notice of me. There were sniggers and jeers from everywhere. I turned to the lady who did all the talking, and said, "My name is Glenyse." She was quite startled; she said, "Oh, dear, I didn't think you had a name."

At the time, I didn't understand what she was

going on about. Mrs. Bigelow came over to me and said in the sweetest voice, "It's all right, dear. You may go to bed now."

This was a shock to my system. I thought, "My luck has changed." At last she felt sorry for me, which stirred my emotions up, as she ushered me out of the room and waited till we got out of hearing distance. "Don't you ever do that to me again!"

I was so taken aback I nearly wet myself. I told her in a very shaky voice that I only wanted to help her. She replied that I had disgraced her in front of all her friends. I went to my room crying with shame and anger.

I lay back on my bed and began to hate the place and the people in it. I wondered what could be so bad about me?

My Attitude

In the morning I got up and did my usual jobs. When I went in to breakfast, she came and told me she was going into town. I was to clean all the party stuff away. I could sense she wasn't happy with me. The feeling was mutual!

While she was in town, she was going to ring the priest up at the mission to tell him of my behaviour, as somehow or other she couldn't quite get through to me. I wasn't doing what she wanted me to do. As far as my work went I was all right, but my attitude towards her . . . she supposed I was very ignorant.

When she left, I sort of shrugged my shoulders. If there was any ignorance, I felt it was on her part, but in those days it was wiser if you didn't say anything. I went about cleaning up the breakfast dishes; then I started in the party room. What a mess that was! It took me all morning to clean and polish, as a lot of drinks had been spilt on the carpet and furniture. They were stained terrible, so I had to do a double cleaning job. Then I went out to the shed to where she kept her wood.

Before leaving, she had ordered me to chop wood and stack the wood boxes up full. When I reached the woodshed, which was near the chook yard, I found the unsplit logs piled right up to the roof. They weren't easy to get at, but I pulled some down, got the axe out from under an old bench, and chopped away at the wood, letting all my frustrations out.

One of her sons was out in a lounge chair, relaxing and reading the paper under a shady tree. It was Robert, the younger one, who seemed more friendly than the rest of them. He did at least answer me when I had to speak to him. That morning I could feel his eyes on me, so I sort of got behind the door a little bit, as I felt shame, bending down and picking up wood in front of him. He must have sensed it too! When I was ready to go into the lounge room with an armload of wood, he beckoned me over to him.

I dropped the wood I was holding and went over to him in a very embarrassed state, wondering what he wanted. I put my head down in a bashful way. He told me he was going to town. Would I go in and polish his shoes?

I didn't even look at him, glad for the chance to get away. I took off to the shoe stand to clean his shoes. When I finished that, I had to place them just outside his bedroom door. Robert was inside and must have heard me. He poked his head out of the doorway, telling me to clean his room up while he was in town. I nodded my head and went on my way down the passage.

In a way I was glad that I would be on my own. I started collecting up the wood again, sort of keeping myself busy until Robert was ready to go. I made sure he could see me working, just in case he met his mother in town. He could let her know that I was toiling very hard when he left.

All the same, I couldn't wait for him to go, as I was dying to raid the fridge and have a good feed, then have a bash at the old piano.

I had learnt to play mainly by teaching myself at the mission. We had singing lessons every Saturday afternoon with Sister Anneburg. She taught us mostly hymns and folk songs—fifty of us at a time gathered around the piano in the dining room.

When the nuns weren't around to stop us, we girls used to slip into the dining room for some practise. That was one good thing about kitchen duties—you could sneak off to the piano. If the nuns were at their prayers, we could have as long as two hours to ourselves having fun and making lots of noise.

I heard the car start up. I waited back in the shed for a while then heard Robert drive off, and I jumped with glee. Cautiously I checked everything out, then went into the kitchen and helped myself to cold meat and salads.

After I cleaned up, I felt very good and at ease. I went into the room where the piano was. I made sure to sit at the window, where I could see down the driveway. Thinking, "This will fix the old girl," I played songs and sang to my heart's content for most of the afternoon. If she could have seen me she would have had a fit!

Then I took a break. I sat back and looked around the room, trying to remember if all my jobs were done, as it was getting late. I got up from the piano and polished all the keys to make sure my fingerprints were not on them.

Then I found an old photo album in her chest of drawers, so I sat back in her rocking chair and browsed through the book. One thing I loved was dwelling on the past of times gone by, of people and places. There seemed to me to be some enchantment about photos and things.

There were photographs of her wedding and of her family when they were younger. So stern and resolute in their looks and dress—even the children looked that way. I had to giggle a bit, as the kids looked so funny, especially the boys in their big baggy shorts and braces. And crew-cut hair. Little did I realize that's how all of us used to look as kids, even more so, as their clothes were in fashion, while ours were way out of fashion.

As I got up to put the book back, I happened to glance down the road. I saw her just getting back into her car after opening the gate. Extremely nervous, I quickly pushed the chair back, checked to see that all was in order, then went out the door quick as a flash, ran to her garden hose, switched it on, and made out I was hard at work watering her garden.

I heard the garage door slam. She came

around to where I was and told me she had a long talk with the priest at the mission, and if my attitude towards her didn't change, I wouldn't be allowed back later on for my holidays. Then she told me to go and collect her shopping from the car and take it into the kitchen.

I was to put all the groceries away and take her personal shopping and put that on her bed; then I was to go out and collect the eggs, as it was getting late. After that I was to set the table for two. She told me not to worry about getting anything to eat for her and her husband. They would have a light meal of salad and cold meat, which she was going to prepare herself. I could have a poached egg—and not to worry about anything else, as her sons were dining out.

While I was eating my poached egg, she came out of the dining room to pick some mail up from the cupboard next to me. Before she went back, she told me that she was going back into town the next day, and would I bake a couple of legs of lamb because the last one seemed to have gone down rather quick, which was unusual. Her sons must be eating very well.

I nearly choked on my last bite of bread. I picked up my tin mug and gulped down some tea, hoping I did not show any signs of being the culprit.

First Pay

As time went by, I was getting used to the place and its surroundings. Mrs. Bigelow went into town quite a lot, which I didn't mind, as I felt quite at ease doing things at my own pace. Strangely enough, I was getting used to her and her ways too. I could control my emotions and not tie myself up with remorseful feelings.

I think her being away all day helped a lot, as I didn't feel so uptight. I used to get very lonely, but I could put up with the loneliness rather than have her around, treating me like a robot.

Whenever she said anything to me, it was like water off a duck's back. I thought the only way to beat her was to give her back some of her own medicine.

One certain day Mrs. Bigelow came to me while I was out in the laundry, washing and scrubbing away on the old scrubbing board. She stated that I had been with her over three months, and this day was Friday, which meant she would take me into town that afternoon, as she was going to pay me for my work. I got very excited, thanked her, and told her that it was nice of her.

When she disappeared back into the house, I lost all interest in the washing, just got it out of the sink and hung it up quickly on the line. I went back into the laundry, then looked back and saw all the soap running from the clothes. The lawn looked like it was snowing.

So I got the water hose which was nearby and hosed the clothes and lawn till all the evidence of soap was gone; then I was off to my room to get ready.

I grabbed my toiletries and had a wash, soaked my head with water; had a quick wipe over with my towel, then went to get dressed. I put on my Sunday best clothes that I used to wear in the mission. Sunday, the nuns considered this day a holy day, a special day, something important to do with their Catholic religion. All usual activities used to cease and we had to dress up in our Good Clothes.

So on this occasion I put on my green pleated skirt, which came down to the ankles; my white blouse with green embroidery around the collar, that matched up with my skirt; got the comb, and ran it through my hair. I put on a pair of pale-yellow shoes, which looked as if they had seen better days, then ran out to where she was waiting in the car.

I opened the front door, apologized for keeping her waiting, then sat down beside her in the front seat. She looked at me in a most disdainful way. Her hands went out towards me in a striking manner, shooing me out of the car. I got the fright of my life, my nerves being in a dreadful state. I thought a spider or lizard was on the seat with us, as she was acting like she was shooing a chook out of her car.

I jumped out of the car, tripped over, and landed in her garden in the most embarrassing state. My skirt was up near my head. I got up quickly and pulled it down, very ashamed that she had seen my bloomers.

I didn't know what to do; I just stood there motionless while she was wiping down the front seat of the car where I had been sitting. When she finished, she told me to go and dry my hair properly, as it was still dripping, then to come back and sit in the backseat of the car—as she never allowed her slaves to sit with her in the front. I went back to my room. I didn't feel like going to town after that episode.

In town I felt strange, as I'd never seen so many people pushing here and there. She told me she was going to the bank, and I was to wait for her in the car till she came back with the money.

I felt nervous sitting there in the car, with people going up and down. It all seemed so frightening. So I got out of the car and ran behind Mrs. Bigelow. When she got to the front door of the bank, I was right beside her, smiling.

She was just about to scold me when her angry face turned into smiles. One of her friends came up and said hello to her. I stood there feeling good, as she couldn't speak to me but had to continue her conversation with her friend. Then she excused herself and explained she was taking me, her dark helper, into the bank, and she would catch up with her later on.

So we went into the bank. I was really terrified as I went up to the counter with her. There were faces, faces everywhere, staring!

The man came to the counter and said, "May I help you, Mrs. Bigelow?" She explained to him that she would like to draw some money out and also that she would like me to open a bank account, so when I came into town next time I could come and get my own money out. She asked the man to fix my business up first. While he went away to get my book and attend to the details, she gave me a fortnight's wages, four pounds.

With trembling hands I folded it up real small and put it in my bra. She told me I wasn't being ladylike and to get myself a purse. I was wishing that the man would hurry up, as I wanted to get out of the place.

At last the man came back. He asked Mrs. Bigelow for all the information. She told him she owed me two months' wages, which was sixteen pounds. She handed him the money to put in the book—then all of a sudden he asked me what my name was.

I put my hands over my face, and with my head down I started to dig up the carpet with my right foot. I was too ashamed to talk to him, as I could hear people walking all around me.

Mrs. Bigelow just got my papers and filled them in, told the man that everything would be all right, and marched me out of the bank. She told me she was disgusted with me, and said to meet her back at the car in half an hour. I was glad I was out of that bank.

So with my four pounds I walked off down the street to see what I could buy. I wasn't going to let her dampen my feelings. It was my first payday, and I was excited that I could buy what I wanted, even though I felt insecure walking around in that strange town.

People walked past and said hello. I turned my head the other way, too bashful to answer back.

I went in search for a shop which sold lollies and chocolates and found one on the corner. There I stood at the door and knocked on it. No one came out, so I knocked on it again. Then, all of a sudden, two high-school kids just about knocked me over as they pushed past to open the door and enter. They turned to me and said, "You don't knock on the door, dumb grannie. You go in and the doorbell rings."

The door slammed in my face. I opened it up and went inside. I stepped over to the counter and looked at the lollies, thinking, "Dumb's not the word!"

I was startled out of my thoughts when a lady asked me in a very gentle voice if there was something I wanted. I went all shy again, put my head down, and started rubbing the floor again with my foot.

What made it worse, I heard those same boys giggling. Then the woman told them not to be so rude, and ordered them to leave. They went out the door, saying "See you, dumbo"—still laughing.

She told me not to worry about those boys, and asked me where I came from. She told me to come over and sit at the table with her, which I did. I was starting to feel at ease. I felt I wanted to cry; I picked up the hem of my skirt and started rolling it up all the time she spoke.

I told her that I came from a mission and was working for Mrs. Bigelow. She told me not to take any notice of her attitude and just do my work, as a lot of girls had worked for Mrs. Bigelow and they had all felt the same way as I did. She told me that she wasn't too keen on her ladyship either: She'd had a couple of run-ins with my employer's husband, as he was the Lord Mayor and disagreed with her on matters concerning the shop. Then she told me if I ever needed a friend, I could come to her anytime and sit down and have a talk.

I thanked her. Then she asked me if I wanted to buy something. I told her I would like to buy a chocolate and a bag of mixed lollies, a pack of biscuits, and a bottle of cool drink.

While she wrapped them up, I got up and took my money from my bra and gave it to her. She gave me all my stuff and two pounds change back, and told me, "Don't worry about nothing"—she'd see me next time I came into town.

I went out of her shop feeling much better,

glad at the thought that I had found a friend in whom I could confide. I made my way back up the street to where Mrs. Bigelow had her car parked.

When I reached her car, she wasn't there, so I sat down on a bench under a tree, and thought I'd have myself a piece of chocolate while I was waiting. It tasted lovely—this was the first time that I had ever tasted chocolate in my life. Then I saw her coming, so I put everything back into the bag, and got up and stood at the back door of the car.

When she reached it, she told me to grab her shopping and put it in the boot of the car. I took the key off her to open the boot, then handed it back straightaway. She opened the doors up, and by that time I'd finished packing all her goods away. I made sure the lid of the boot was down secure; then I climbed in the backseat of the car.

She didn't say much to me. I was getting quite used to her attitude. I was thinking I couldn't wait for next time to come into town, as I had found a friend, and she was nothing like Mrs. Bigelow!

Wash the Car Seat

As we sped back home, I sat back and viewed the scenery, which was very pretty. The big hills and the winding road, the erectness of the gum trees—a perfect picture of nature.

All too soon we were in front of the gate leading up to her farm. I got out to open it as she drove through. She told me to get back into the car and leave the gate open. We drove up to the house, and she said she would leave the car in the driveway, as she wanted me to wash the seat I had been sitting on with Pine-o-cleen before she parked it in the garage. After that I was to take her shopping into her room, then get on with my other jobs.

So I went to my room, put my small bag on my bed, got changed out of my good clothes, and put my working clothes on. Then I set about finding the Pine-o-cleen to give the car a thorough wash.

I just emptied the bottle all over the car's front and back seats. The smell was very strong and sickening, so I stood back from the car a bit to breathe in some fresh air. Then I took a rag and

the running hose into the car and sloshed it out.
When that was finished, I went over to check
her shopping to see if anything had gotten wet,
because the car was right next to the verandah
and there was water everywhere.

While I was checking, I thought I might as
well take her shopping to her room. Fortunately
it was dry. Just as I was bending down to pick
it up, she stepped out onto the verandah,
grabbed her bags out of my hands, and asked
me why all this water was running everywhere.

I told her I was only doing what she wanted
me to do, and that was wash her car. She
walked over to the car and took a look inside.
She nearly had a fit when she saw how soaked
and wet everything was. She looked at me in a
furious state and called me "a very stupid girl!"
and if I damaged any upholstery in her car she
was taking it out of my wages. I was to hurry
up and get this mess all cleaned up. She told
me she had asked me to wipe over my seat with
a cloth, not drench the car.

After it was dried out, she parked the car in
the garage, and I finished watering her lawn and
gardens, then went inside to set her table and
get the meal ready for her. She was there in the
lounge chair, sitting and reading the paper. She
told me she had a casserole in the fridge. I was
to put that in the oven to warm it up; then, when
it was ready, I was to let her know, as by that
time Mr. Bigelow should be back from town,
and I could take their tea in to them and serve

it up. She said I could have bread and butter and open up a tin of spaghetti for my tea.

While I was waiting for the casserole to heat up, I pottered around getting my tea ready. I was in the kitchen when Mr. Bigelow drove up, so I went to check the casserole—it was piping hot. I turned the oven off and made sure everything was ready. Then I heard her call out to bring the tea in and serve it up. So I laid the trolley up and went into the lounge to serve them.

While I was there, she told me, tomorrow being Saturday, her and Mr. Bigelow would be out all day, and her boys would be gone for the weekend too, so I was to make sure all their shoes were clean and spotless. I was to make sure to round up all the turkeys and lock them in their yard, as the foxes were starting to get at them again. I was also to collect the eggs and stack them away in a container. "Next time I go to town I will take them with me, as a friend of mine is asking for some. Then you know the old shed at the end of the garden? I want you to give it a good clean out."

The list went on. "Also you will find some boxes under a ledge. In those boxes you'll find some preserving jars. Get all the jars—there are about five dozen—I want you to give them a thorough washing and cleaning, because next week I shall be preserving some more fruit. The pears are beginning to ripen and we are quite short of them. When you have completed those jobs, you can go down to the orchard and pick some pears for the table—fill the fruit bowl up!

"Then you can cook Mr. Bigelow and myself some tea: We will have chops and vegies." She asked if I understood everything—then added that instead of sweeping the driveway first thing in the morning, I was to go down and pick her oranges. She would like her juice at seven o'clock, as she was going out at eight.

I left the room and went to have my tea, which I was thankful for, as I was feeling rather washed out with all those orders and jobs, though in another sense of my thinking, I was glad that they were all going out—I was looking forward to a very peaceful day!

So after I had my tea and Mr. and Mrs. Bigelow retired to the lounge, I got stuck into the cleaning up. When all my duties were done, I went to bed feeling quite knocked out.

Shadows on the Wall

In the morning I woke up still feeling quite drained out. I dressed rather wearily, as the way I was feeling I could have slept for a week. "Maybe after a good wash I'll feel better," I thought.

So I got the old burner down, lit it up, and armed with my towel and soap, I set off to the old washtub. I had myself a good wash and felt much better. When I went out to get the straw broom, I noticed it was still quite dark. Suddenly I remembered she wanted me to go down to the paddock where the orange tree was and pick two oranges for her. I didn't feel like going, as I was a bit scared.

When I was a little girl growing up in the mission, I had this great fear of the dark, as the big girls used to tell us little girls ghostie yarns and how the devil was out to get us. Also the nuns would lock us in dark rooms at night, which terrified me.

I remember how at the mission, when the lights used to go out at nine o'clock in the dormitory, the nuns used to leave an old lantern burning in the fireplace. If anyone wanted to go to the toilet at night she had to walk towards that lantern, up the long passage.

The closer she came, the bigger the shadow on the wall grew. And when she leaned over to pick it up, her shadow bent down too. We got the feeling that our days were up; we just about wet ourself on the spot.

Also I remember telling the girls a joke after lights-out in the dormitory, one I heard that day in school. I did not know it was dirty because we were never taught about the birds and the bees. My sister and I used to fight like cats and dogs, and she dobbed me in.

If you were caught talking after lights-out, you had to take the consequences, so rather than be locked up in the dark, I told this nun the joke. She dropped her bundle of keys in shock and told me they never heard these jokes in Germany! So I took my hiding rather than be locked up. To this day I am still very frightened of the dark.

This particular morning I thought I'd be brave and not think about anything. I'd just go straight down and back. Nothing to it! I got the lantern, set my fears aside, and off I went. The wind was blowing the leaves in all directions. It was stronger as I got further down the track. A couple of times the flame nearly went out. I was starting to get shivers down my back, but I kept on walking till I reached the big fence. I put the lantern in a position where the light shone faintly on the orange tree.

Now I was over the fence, making my way there, when I heard this movement like something scratching the ground. I looked up, and right in front of me, under the orange tree, I saw this big woolly ram ready to charge. I let out one big scream, and I was back over that fence in no time.

The lantern went out. I didn't wait to pick it up; I left it there next to the fence. Like a hunted doe with her heart full of fear, I bounded back to the house and never once looked back.

I went into the garage, turned on the big lights, and sat there till I caught my breath.

Now that I had got my breath back, and I was my normal self again, I wondered what to do about her orange juice. No way was I going back down there again. So what I thought I'd do was go into the kitchen, get two oranges, and squeeze the juice out of them.

So I went quietly into the kitchen. Nobody was up yet. Quickly I rushed around and got her orange juice ready. I went into the lounge, got her glass out, poured the juice in, put a clean doyley over it, cleaned my mess up, then went outside. I felt good now, as it was beginning to get light. Before I started sweeping, I thought I'd better go and get the lantern, as I did not want to explain anything to her. So I ran down to get it.

That horrible old ram was still there. Before I knew what I was doing, I picked up a rock and threw it to get even with him. I collected the lantern and went back to sweep her driveway.

I made sure everything was done before she got up. I wanted to be in the kitchen then, because I remembered she had said she was getting up early, and if I was outside, she would start asking questions, as it should not take that long for my outside jobs to be completed. So having swept her driveway, I went into the kitchen, glad that she was not up yet. I set her table for breakfast, then put the kettle on.

By this time it was ten to seven. As she came in, I said, "Good morning," and as usual got no answer. I was asked where had I put her orange juice. I told her it was on her breakfast table. She told me to go and get it, as she would have it in the kitchen.

She drank it down, then shuddered with distaste, her wrinkles tightening up on her old face. "Oh, that was very bitter. The sweet oranges must be just about all gone," she said.

I continued on with my duties as if I did not know anything about it. She told me, "When you go down to the orchard, you'll find an old man there working. Could you ask him to pick a bag of sweet oranges off the tree? He'll know what kind I want, and what tree to pick them from. Then bring them up to the house and put them in the pantry. I'll have two of those every morning.

"And now that you have been here over three months, you can do all the cooking. I'll leave a menu in the kitchen on the wall so that you can follow what meals we are having during the week. The main meals will be breakfast, and tea at night, when we are all together. Don't worry about dinner so much, as most of the time we won't be here. If the boys are not going to be here for any of our meals, I'll let you know.

"You can start by cooking bacon and eggs for our breakfast. We'll have our eggs medium, and for a change, we'll have coffee, so you can put the percolator on."

She left me there feeling rather breathless. Every time she came over to talk to me, I was beginning to feel a sense of debility creeping over me. I set about the task of getting their breakfast ready. The bacon and eggs smelt scrumptious, making my mouth water.

After I dished their breakfast up on a plate, I purposely left the pan near the stove. I had no intentions of cleaning it, as I was going to have a good fry-up when they left. I made the toast, put it on the toast racks; then, as everything was prepared, I went in to see if they were ready to eat.

Mr. Bigelow was there going through some papers, so I went into the kitchen, loaded the trolley up, and took everything into the dining room. I took the breakfast off the trolley, set it down on the table, then checked to see if nothing was missing and all was in place. I had forgotten the serviettes! So I quickly went to the drawer to get the rings out, polished them, then rolled the serviettes up and slipped them in the rings, which I placed on their individual plates.

Feeling quite pleased about getting breakfast ready all by myself, I turned to Mr. Bigelow, who by now had finished going through his papers. I said to him, "Breakfast is ready," then walked out, knowing full well that I wouldn't get a reply.

I went about cleaning the kitchen. When everything was tidy, I sat down to have my plate of weeties, thinking, "This is not the only thing I am going to eat this morning."

I carried on in my normal way so as not to arouse suspicions if she were to come into the kitchen—which she did, to tell me off for taking breakfast in when she wasn't present in the dining room.

I apologized and explained to her that, when I saw Mr. Bigelow sitting at the table, I naturally thought he was waiting for his breakfast. She carried on in her usual tone. I was to wait till she rang the bell, and if ever there was a time that Mr. Bigelow was on his own, I wasn't to go in. It wasn't very nice for a slave girl to be all alone in the presence of a male member of the family.

She asked me how much coffee had I put in the percolator. Seeing that it was my first effort in making coffee, especially in a percolator—I had never set eyes on one before—I felt rather pleased. For once I thought she was going to praise me up, for making good coffee, but my sense of her good intentions soon became dispirited, when I told her I poured half a tin of coffee into the percolator.

"You are a very stupid girl! You need only to put a couple of dessert spoons in. Now hop up and make a fresh one!"

So I left my breakfast and followed her into the dining room to get the coffee pot.

I had been stunned by the comment she made about being alone with her husband. I couldn't understand it. To make it look good, I immediately went into the dining room with the trolley and made myself busy. I had other intentions on my mind as soon as they would leave.

Now I was out in the kitchen again, washing up the dishes, when I heard her yoohoo. Whenever she was at home, or if I was outside doing things, or she couldn't see me, she had a habit of yoohooing out to me, like she was out in the paddock, trying to round up a horse or something.

I went running to see what she wanted. She told me I was to go get Mr. Bigelow's shoes from the shoe rack and make sure they were clean and shining.

So I ran out to get his shoes. They looked brand-new, as I always made sure that all shoes were kept cleaned, because with my heavy workload I had a fear of being scolded if the other jobs were not done on time. So I quickly grabbed his shoes and ran back into the house with them and put them down on the floor outside their bedroom.

She briskly came out of the room and told

me to pick the shoes up and pass them to her in the proper manner, as it wasn't in her category to bend down and pick things up from the floor. I apologized and went on into the kitchen, to continue my cleaning duties.

While I was busy in the dining room polishing up the silverware and brassware from the mantelpiece to the window ledges, which were spread around the room, I caught a glimpse of them strutting past the window. The way they were both dressed reminded me of the characters out of a book I used to read when I was a child, called *The Three Musketeers*.

I picked up an item I was polishing and moved towards a window from where I could follow the car with my eyes right down the driveway. When it turned left onto the highway to go into town, I dropped what I was doing, sat back, and gave a sigh of relief.

The Turkeys

Mm, just to smell the aroma of bacon and eggs cooking made my mouth water. Then I made some toast, and when everything was ready, I got my old tin plate and tin mug, chucked them in the sink, and took out a setting from one of her finest crockery services. I went into the dining room where she sat at the table, laid everything out, got a clean serviette, put that on my bread-and-butter plate, then went into the kitchen to get my breakfast out of the oven.

Just as I was about to sit down, I had a feeling that there was something missing. "Oh, yes, that's it!" So I went to the boys' room and got the wireless out. "I'll have some music. The place is a bit quiet and needs livening up." I turned the music up loud and then sat down to the most nourishing meal of my life—all the time thinking, "If she could see me now, she'd probably have a heart attack."

I felt quite contented just sitting there enjoying my breakfast. "Well, why not?" I thought.

"I work hard, and it's about time I took it easy for a while."

Now that I had demolished everything on my plate, I felt quite satisfied. "That breakfast was sufficient," I thought to myself. "I'll just skimp through my main jobs that have to be done; she won't know any better."

When everything looked fresh and clean, I could take a walk and look for the turkeys. It was such a nice day outside, a pity to stay indoors and work. So I went into her old shed and found a big stick in the corner.

One of my childhood habits was to always walk along with a stick in my hand. We did a lot of bush walking when I was in the mission, and the nuns could never understand why we used to all grab our sticks when we set off for the bush, as they came along with us. I guess it gave us a sense of security.

Now that I had my stick in my hand, I set off in the direction of the orchard, thinking it would be nice if I had some ripe, juicy pears and apples to munch on during my walk through the paddocks.

So off I went, down to the orchard. When I got there, I opened up the big iron gates and made my way down a few lanes, selecting out the best fruit. I couldn't wait to sample that fruit. I sunk my teeth into a big juicy pear.

Never before in my growing years did I have the opportunity to help myself to fresh fruit, so I might as well make the most of it while I could.

In the mission we only saw fresh fruit once in a blue moon. I remember when we were little girls, we used to sneak around the convent to where the nuns used to have their meals and hide and wait in the grass until one of the nuns emptied the scraps in the bin. We used to wait for the right moment; then it would be one mad dash to the bins to get the orange and apple peels out.

I remember the big silent fights we used to have unbeknown to the nuns. If they had realised, we would've got a flogging for sure.

I smiled to myself as I took off my apron, put my fruit into it, then bundled it up in knapsack style, threw it over my shoulder, and went off down towards the river, as that's where she said I would find her turkeys.

As I went along, I looked all around at the countryside, which was very hilly. The gullies were steep and deep. "Fascinating," I thought as I climbed up onto a big log and looked all around me. Far off in the distance I could see the rooftops of different farmhouses spread out on the horizon. Different shades of green lay everywhere.

"Lovely," I thought as I jumped down from the log and set about searching for the turkeys and eggs. I was looking forward to a nice cup of tea and a piece of sponge cake with cream, which I had seen in the fridge.

It didn't take me long to find the turkeys, as I heard their gobbles in a clump of grass near the riverbed. They were strutting around, looking most conceited.

All of a sudden the quietness of the air was filled with loud gobbling noises, as feathers and birds went flying in all directions. I had my stick out shooing them in the direction of the house when out of the blue this big cheeky turkey came towards me and made a peck at my legs. I got a fright and screamed and, in reaction, brought my stick down hard across his neck. He slumped to the ground.

My heart was still pumping flat out from the fright I got, so I went back to the house to have a cup of tea to settle my nerves.

When I reached the house, I went straight into the kitchen and put the kettle on. I made my cup of tea and sat down with a sigh of relief. "Ah, that cup of tea was just what I needed, and that cream cake went down real well too."

There was still an hour left before midday, so I thought I'd better have another go at rounding the turkeys up and locking them in the yard; then she couldn't say anything to me when she got home. So away I went again. They were all in the same spot where I had hit the turkey. It was still on the ground. They all scattered when I went to poke that big cheeky one with my stick.

It didn't move, and a dreadful thought crossed my mind. "What if the bird is dead? It is my fault. I killed it. Oh, gosh, what's going to happen now? How am I going to explain this one to her when she gets back from town?"

Being brought up in a strict environment, I

was never allowed to tell lies; but since I had been working there for her, I found myself really good at it. So I told myself I'd think of something to tell her.

I still felt disheartened about the whole affair. I left the turkeys to roam around: I'd get them another day. "The only way to get rid of the dead one," I thought, "is to bury it!" So I ran as fast as I could back to the old shed, got the spade, and ran back to the river where the turkey lay.

I dug a big hole and chucked it in, covered it all up, put some bushes over the top to hide all the evidence, then went back up to the house, washed all the sand off, and put the spade back where I got it from.

I felt real horrible. I had never done anything like that in my whole life. I walked slowly into the kitchen and glanced at the clock on the wall. The time was showing eleven thirty. I didn't feel like eating, as I had lost my appetite thinking about that unfortunate turkey. I wished I had never set eyes on it. I sat down on the chair in the kitchen with a feeling of emptiness. I was beginning to let my emotions get the better of me, feeling homesick.

At least if there were other kids around, with whom I could share a laugh and a joke. Maybe if I had one of my mates with me, the episode of the turkey wouldn't seem so bad. We could look on the funny side of it and have a good laugh.

Tears welled up in my eyes. I just let them

splash down onto the floor as I cried uncontrollably. It was such a long time since I had a good cry. All of a sudden the phone rang. I jumped up and pulled myself to my senses.

I washed my face at the kitchen sink and dried my eyes. The phone was still ringing, so I went into the dining room, and then I suddenly remembered that she didn't want me to answer the phone.

I stood in front of it, not knowing what to do. I just stared at it till it stopped ringing. Then I went back into the kitchen feeling a lot better since I'd had that cry.

My Old Tin Mug

I went to the fridge and thought I'd better have something to eat after all, as I was starting to feel a bit weak—and peckish. I cut myself a big piece of ham, a piece of mutton, and a piece of silverside, topped my plate up with salads, then decided that I'd have my meal in the dining room again with all the trimmings.

It was only when I went into the pantry to get the pickles that I remembered that she wanted me to go and get the rest of the preserving jars from the old shed. I looked on the shelf where she kept her jars of preserved fruit. There were only a couple of jars of plums and pears left. The shelf looked quite bare, so I thought I'd have my lunch first, then after I'd get stuck into that job.

So I sat down at the table and tucked into my dinner. When I'd finished, I went and helped myself to plums and ice cream for sweets. I couldn't bear not having any plums. As soon as I saw them, I had to have some, they looked so scrumptious—they were my favourite fruit, too.

After dinner, I cleaned up my mess, made

sure everything was neat and tidy, then went out to the shed to fetch the jars. I hated going into that shed. It was so dark and miserable. Every time I opened up the door, it used to make me squirm and go all goose-bumpy. The first things I used to think of were snakes and spiders. There were cobwebs everywhere; they hung in all directions. Oh, it used to feel real spooky!

Every time I sneezed, I used to have to wait a couple of seconds till the thick cloud of dust settled down to get my bearings; and the screeching of the old wooden door when I opened it up used to send cold shivers down my spine.

This old shed was situated right down the bottom end of her garden, which was at the back of her house, and it nestled in between two very old lemon trees. It reminded me of a witches' den.

There was no lighting in the shed. I had to light up the old burner to see. The window had boards nailed over it.

As I struck a match to light up the lamp, her two cats came strolling by. They must have been curious as to what I was doing. They were friendly cats, so I sang out, ''Puss, puss!'' They came bounding over to me in a playful manner and rubbed themselves up against my legs as I bent down to stroke them.

I picked up the two cats and put them down on the shed floor. I did not feel too bad with the cats there, as I knew they had a good sense of danger. So if anything was in there, I'd leave them to kill it, whether it was a spider or snake, because I wouldn't be around—I'd be gone like the wind!

I stooped down to have a look on the bottom shelves for the jars, as I couldn't see them on the higher ones. I spotted them right at the back row, down low. She had them packed in boxes—six boxes there were. I crouched to make it a bit easier for myself, as there was a lot of junk in front of them.

As I cleaned all the junk away, and was still in a crouching position, just reaching to grab a box of jars, one of the cats landed in my lap from the top shelf. All I could think of was a snake. I went all cold and just about screamed the place down. That cat got more of a fright than I did. I didn't mean to half kill it when I picked it up out of my lap and flung it. The poor thing landed up against the wall. The other cat just disappeared.

I went around to the front of the house to calm my nerves, still shaking terribly. I glanced at the colourful flowers and reached out, with my hands trembling, to touch one beautiful pink bloom when I heard this voice say, "Good day, lassie."

I turned around quickly to face the gentleman who spoke. Here in this place I found it very strange for someone to be speaking to me as if he was sort of interested in me as a person. Since being on the farm, I felt like a robot.

None of the Bigelow family really talked to me, and on the days that she was around, she would either address me as "Are you there?" or yoohoo out to me. So I got to feel like it was wrong for anyone to talk to me, and when they did speak to me, I would just look at them dumbfounded. Then if I did speak back to them, I became very conscience stricken.

So when this old gentleman spoke to me—I was always taught that all men were gentlemen—I put my fears aside, as I didn't want to let him know that I was just getting over a fright. I turned to him and noticed he had a couple of buckets of fruit. His face was covered in wrinkles and his eyes were blue and misty, but there was something about him that I took a liking to.

He must have noticed the expression on my face, for he told me not to be worried. He explained to me that he worked in the orchard for the Bigelows. He had worked for them for years, and was just bringing some fruit up as this was the time of the year that she did her bottling. He said to me, "You must be the new lass?" I said, "Yes." He asked me where I came from, and I told him, "A place called Wandering Mission."

He told me I wasn't the first one. There were girls coming and going all the time and from different homes. Then he said, if I'd go and open up the kitchen door for him, he'd carry the fruit in for me, which was very nice of him. I thanked him, and I told him I was just getting the jars ready for the fruit.

So we made our way into the kitchen. He put

the fruit in the sink for me. I was longing to have a good old yarn to him, as he was the kind of person who made me feel differently from the rest of those around the farm. So I asked him if he would like a cup of tea. He said that he usually brought his flask of tea to work, but today for some reason or other had forgotten it. He lived on his own.

He had an old shack on the other side of town, and sometimes, he explained, he forgot things, but seeing I offered, he'd love one. So I asked him to sit down on one of the chairs in the kitchen. He sat down while I got things ready. I felt his gaze on me as I moved around.

Suddenly he said, "Lassie, you look so young. How old are you?" "I am sixteen," I said. "Why, child, where are your mum and dad?" I told him, "I have a mum, but I don't know where she is. I'll find her one day, I suppose. My dad I have never seen. He died when I was in the home." I explained to him how we were taken away from our natural parents as babies and that we grew up in the care of Catholic nuns, priests, and brothers, and when we got to the age of sixteen, they sent us out to places like this to work for people.

As I put the pot of tea on the table, I thought I'd better use my tin mug in front of this dear old gentleman. When on my own I used a cup and saucer, nobody knew, it was my secret! Even though he was a nice old gentleman, I thought I'd do the right thing. I put a cup and saucer in front of him and put my old tin mug on the table. He thanked me and I went to the fridge, cut two pieces of cake, and put them on the table.

When one of the pussycats meowed and brushed up against me, I picked him up and gave him a cuddle, as this was the poor cat I had chucked up against the wall. Glad to know that it was well and not hurt, I bent down to place the cat on the floor.

The old man said, "Hey, lassie, the pussy sure knows when it's cup-of-tea time." He reached out to grab my tin mug and said, "Here, pass over the milk and I'll fill up his tin mug."

I hesitated, as I fumbled to pick up the milk. He had a look of concern on his face as he asked me what was wrong. I felt my face go all sorts of colours as I explained to him that the tin mug was the cup which I had to drink from, as the boss of the house said I was not to use her stuff. He flung his old grey head back and gave out one big laugh.

I stood there trembling, feeling real stupid, when all of a sudden his wrinkled face turned serious, and he said, "Lassie, you are not playing any jokes on me?"

I was very near to tears as I plucked up courage and told him that the boss gave me orders to drink out of a tin mug and eat off an old tin plate. He realised then I was serious and asked me what were her reasons. I told him that she said I am her slave!

With a look of mystification about his old

face, he spoke in a very gentle voice and told me to go and get a cup and saucer and sit down and have a cup of tea with him. He explained to me that he would be my friend if I needed one. He couldn't understand why people should be treated the way they were. It was very unfair and unjust. We chatted on a bit more and when I told him that I had to go to the old shed and get the six boxes of bottles, he offered to come and help me.

On our way down he told me, whenever the boss was away and I had a job I couldn't handle, I was to come down to the orchard and look for him. If I couldn't see him, I was to come over and look in his car, where he would probably be having a smoke. He parked his old green ute right down near the river end. I could spot it through her bedroom window, as that was the highest part of the house.

As we got down to the shed, I felt very happy that I had found a friend and also glad that it wasn't me in that old shed getting the bottles. He sang out to tell me the boxes were all rotten, so what he would do was take the jars out separately and put them on the lawn. What I could do was go and turn the hose on and wash all the jars out on the lawn, as they were very dirty and dusty. When all the bottles were clean, he helped me carry them into the kitchen, and we stacked them on the empty shelves.

Everything was done, and I warmly thanked him for all his help. As I handed him his buckets, he told me to call him Bill and not to forget—if ever I needed him, I knew what to do. He told me to keep smiling and not to worry about anything, then made his way back to the orchard.

I had a real light sensation come over me as I went back into the kitchen. I looked at the pears and apples on the sink, then at the clock. It was five minutes past four. "Gee," I thought, "how the time went quick today."

Another two hours and the boss would be back. I still had a couple of jobs to do. First, peel all the fruit and cut it up, then go out and water all the gardens, the front and back, then go and collect the eggs, then back into the house to get things ready for their tea.

I thought while I was peeling the fruit that I'd go and turn on the sprinklers at the back and the front. In that way the gardens and lawn could be getting a good watering while I got on with my other jobs. It would save some time.

I didn't know why she couldn't let me use those sprinklers when she was there. It would have made watering much easier for me. So having done that, I went back into the kitchen to peel and cut the fruit, only stopping to go out and change the sprinklers.

I had completed all my jobs and still had half an hour up my sleeve, so I went to check the gardens. I made sure every part had plenty of water, and put the sprinklers away so there would be no questions asked on their arrival back, which I hated. The feelings of remorse came sinking back inside me.

Shoosh, Shoosh, Girl!

As I was setting the table for supper, I looked out the window and saw the car coming up the driveway.

I was pottering around putting the finishing touches to the table and tea trolley when I heard the kitchen door open. She came in to me and said, "Ah, there you are. Could you go out to the car and bring the shopping in? You can take my personal shopping and put it on the bed. Bring the groceries in first and put them away. In the meantime I'll cook the chops, as my sons will be home for tea and I know how they like them. You can put the vegies on. We will have potatoes, spinach, and carrots. When I've cooked the chops, I'll leave you to it.

"And when the vegies are cooked, I want you to mash the potatoes, then put the vegies in separate bowls. Come and let me know when all is ready. Then we will have our tea, as by that time the boys should be back from town. You can open up a can of baked beans for your tea."

So I left her cooking her chops, and I went

to attend to my job of putting her shopping away. I took her new personal things and chucked them on her bed, glad of the fact that Mr. Bigelow wasn't in the room, as I dreaded having to face him. I didn't like the way he used to just stare at me. I used to feel so embarrassed!

I went back out to the car to get the groceries. I collected the three bags she had and went into the kitchen with them. I put them on the table and started to sort the shopping out, separating all the cleaning things—Ajax, Pine-o-cleen, Silvo, Brasso, etc., to make it easier for me. Then, when everything was sorted, I just grabbed whatever belonged to where and put everything away without any mixup. By this time she was out in the lounge reading the papers, so I got stuck into putting the vegies on.

By the time the tea was cooked, it was seven thirty, so I went in to tell her everything was ready to be served up. As usual I got told off for barging in and not knocking. Her sons were there with her.

I apologized. She told me to put everything on the trolley, wheel it into the dining room, and leave it. "Put the sweets on too. We will have peaches and cream. Don't worry about making tea. We'll have a late cup of tea when you have gone to bed. Mr. Bigelow is complaining that you make the tea too strong, which reminds me, I'll have to give you a lesson in making tea one of these days."

Then she told me, "Go and bring everything

in, leave it, then shut the door, as the family does not want any interruptions.''

Having done that, I was feeling very hurt as I went to open up my can of baked beans. While I was waiting for them to warm up, I got my tin plate out and a fork, then sat down at the table. I must have been lost in thought when I saw steam coming out of the saucepan. I jumped up and poured the beans out on my plate, feeling rather worn out. I didn't feel like eating. I sort of just sat there picking away at my meal.

I didn't mind if she told me off when no one was around, but she had a habit of always reprimanding me when all the rest of the family was there. I used to get so ashamed, as I could feel all their eyes on me. I was beginning to really detest it!

One of these days I'd pluck up courage and tell her how I felt—not that it would make any difference, but at least I would have my say.

In the midst of my reflections I heard the bell ringing, so I got up and made my way into the dining room, feeling rather gloomy, as no doubt they'd all be staring at me and she'd be there like a cat ready to pounce on her prey.

I carried on collecting dishes and stacking them on the trolley; then she banged on her table with her serviette ring. ''Shoosh, shoosh, girl!'' I looked at her. ''You are making far too much noise; go a bit steady.''

She stood up, put the remaining dishes on the trolley, and in a rude and abrupt manner ushered me out of the room, then slammed the door. ''Ouch!''—in that mad dash out of the dining room door, one of the wheels of the trolley had gone over my foot.

I sat down on my chair in the kitchen to grab at my foot and rub it a bit to relieve the pain that surged through it. All of a sudden, while I was sitting on the chair nursing my foot, the door opened up. She rushed out to put a plate down on the table. The look on her face when she saw me sitting there—I thought she was going to have a heart attack.

''How dare you sit down when you have work to do! You put that horrible old thong on your foot and get up and start the dishes. I won't tolerate this behaviour, especially coming from my slave. Now do you understand that?''

I burst out crying and leapt up, nearly wetting myself. Mrs. Bigelow just went on shouting at me, ''You go out to your sink and wash your face, and stop that stupid nonsense! I don't want all that muck falling into the washing-up water. Now go on, get a move on!''

I couldn't wait to get out of the kitchen quick enough. While I freshened up my face at my own washhouse sink, I started to tremble. Gosh, what would her reaction be if she found out I killed a turkey? The way she felt about me, I was more determined that she wasn't going to find out.

So I slowly made my way back into the kitchen. She was waiting there for me, writing something down on a piece of paper. She

looked at me and told me that she would be
going back into town the next day, which was
Wednesday, and wanted more fruit bottled.

I was to peel as much fruit as possible, cut
it all up, and, with what I had already prepared,
put the lot into jars. I was to top up the fruit-
filled jars with sugar and water, then stand them
along the cupboard. "Tomorrow night when I
come home, I'll start to cook them in the pre-
server." Then it came. "Also, I was meaning
to ask you, did you manage to get the turkeys
and their eggs? I want to take a dozen tomorrow
when I go into town."

I nearly died on the spot, as she had caught
me unaware. I couldn't stop myself from stut-
tering, trying to explain I didn't find any
turkeys.

She told me to stand up straight, stop slouch-
ing, and to face her when she was talking to
me.

I hoped I didn't show any signs of guilt. I felt
my face quivering. When it came to answering
questions face on, I wasn't much good at hiding
my guilt, but I must have done all right this
time. Mrs. Bigelow seemed to be convinced
that I had searched everywhere but to no avail:
I couldn't find them.

She told me not to worry for the time being.
Another job she wanted me to do was go out to
the woodshed and chop the wood again. She
wanted me to chop as much as I could, as the
wood boxes were empty, and of an evening
when the nights were cold it was not good for

Mr. Bigelow to be out collecting wood. He might catch a cold, and she couldn't have him sick. Being Lord Mayor, he had a lot of functions to attend, all very important ones which he could not miss.

"Now, do you understand your instructions?" I said, "Yes, Mrs. Bigelow."

Before she turned to go, she told me to be up half an hour earlier than my usual time, which was five o'clock. She wanted my jobs to be finished early in the morning, as she must have her breakfast served at seven o'clock. She and her husband had to be in town early, and with that she told me to hurry up and finish my work, because I had made enough noise for the evening.

Then she added, "By the way, don't worry about getting breakfast for the boys. They will be going out. If they want breakfast, they'll let you know."

She closed the door behind her and I continued on with my work. It was about half past nine when I shut the kitchen door and went out to my bedroom, glad of the fact that I could at last have a good rest. I felt completely drained out. I struggled to put my nightie on. Oh, what an exhausting day it had been!

Running Whenever She Needed Me

Just as I was about to be attacked by a mob of vicious turkeys, I awoke to the sound of high-pitched ringing. Jolted out of my terrible nightmare, I reached out, grabbed the clock to turn the alarm off, then lit up the old burner. I pulled my towel off the edge of my bed, to wipe the sweat off my face. My heart was still beating fast, and my legs felt as if they had been running all night!

I lay back to let my nerves settle down and to come back to reality with myself. I lay there thinking about what sort of a day I was going to have. I felt real happy that they were going out again. It would give me an opportunity to go down and have a yarn with old Bill. I'd get him to come up and have a cup of tea with me. I might even ask him to help me cut some wood, because the thought of all that chopping made me feel weak. I just wished I knew what time her sons were going out. As soon as they left, I'd head straight down to the orchard.

I thought I'd better hurry up and get started on my jobs. Suddenly, I remembered that she wanted breakfast early. Now that I had shaken that horrible nightmare out of my system, I got myself dressed. Thinking, "It's too cold for a shower," I decided I'd have one later when everyone had left the farm.

I could use her shower room. It was so much nicer and warmer, as her toilet and shower room were in her bedroom. I remembered her powder smelt lovely. I liked the lavender one. I'd put some of that on me after my shower.

As soon as I was dressed, I went to my own washhouse and freshened up my face and combed my hair. Back at my room, I just chucked my toiletries on the bed and slammed the door. Then I grabbed the old burner and broom, intending to start down from the orchard and work my way up to the front, then finish off my chores at the shoe rack. I had to polish their shoes and make sure they were spotless before they left for town.

So I made my way down to the bottom end of the driveway and started sweeping up all the leaves and dust. The wind was blowing hard, and I began to get a bit frustrated. I was fighting a losing battle—the more leaves I swept together, the more the wind would blow them all over the place.

I thought, "I'll just sweep from side to side. Too bad if the wind blows the leaves back again." So I hurried up and made a quick job of it. I put the lantern and broom back where they belonged, then went to the shoe rack to start polishing the shoes.

When I finally finished the shoes, I didn't feel like going all the way down to the paddock to pick her oranges. So I went into my room and got two out of my fruit bowl, which I had picked from the orchard a week before. They were a bit soft, but she wouldn't know. At least there'd be a lot of juice in them. In the kitchen, I took a glass from the cabinet and squeezed the week-old oranges.

Um they were juicy, too! I poured the rich juice into the glass and filled it up. I had a taste to see if the juice was sweet. It tasted all right to me, so I tidied my mess up, put a clean doyley over the glass, then set about getting breakfast.

When I put the bacon and eggs on, I didn't forget myself. If she told me off, I'd just say that I was making some for her sons, too, playing dumb to the fact that she had already explained to me about the boys—besides, I couldn't help the way I was, just a shadow in this mansion. I went into the dining room to set the table up and make sure everything was laid out correctly, then went back into the kitchen. I glanced at the clock. It was about ten minutes to seven. I put the kettle on.

She called out to me from the dining room that she and Mr. Bigelow were ready for their breakfast, but as I was setting up the trolley, she came in to drink her orange juice. The perfume she had on her was very strong, a sickly sort of smell. I caught a good whiff of it as she passed me. Her rouge and makeup always fascinated me. She often looked like she was ready for the circus.

I was just about to take the trolley in when she sort of tugged at the sleeve of my dress and told me that she'd wheel it in. She moved me out of the way abruptly and told me to bring in the bacon, eggs, and toast when she rang the bell. "Don't worry about making coffee. Just put the boiling water in a jug and bring it in with you when I am ready for the main breakfast."

She went into the dining room with the trolley and shut the door behind her, leaving me standing there empty-handed. I thought that I'd better have my cereal, so I got my old tin plate out, filled it up with weeties, poured milk and sugar over them, then began. She rang the bell.

I dropped the spoon, quickly hopped up, got the plates of bacon and eggs, took them into the dining room, placed them on their individual places, then stood back to see if there was anything else she wanted before I went back into the kitchen.

As I stood there, I got a fit of the sniffles and took out my old rag, which I had tucked in my sleeve jumper, and blew into it in a most profound manner, making the most peculiar noise.

She stood up in a very angry mood and told me to leave the room at once. What I had done was very rude—to blow my nose in front of decent citizens like her and her husband. If I happened to do it again, she was going to report me to the priest at the mission. This was one thing she would not tolerate, especially from her servant. I shook as I made my way out to the kitchen.

Every time she scolded me I felt like I was dirt; but as I explained before, I sort of overlooked the situation. I could see the funny side of things. I was a person that nothing could ever get down for long. I was a happy-go-lucky girl!

Sometimes when she scolded me, I thought she was quite comical, but I never dared laugh in front of her. It was always at the back of her, or when she was out of my sight.

Even when the nuns scolded me at the mission, I could always see the funny side, especially when my mates were around me. We used to think it was a big joke to be slapped and told off. I mean, we wouldn't laugh straightaway, but only afterwards when we caught up with one another in the dining room or kitchen. We'd look at one another, and that was it! We'd have a good old laugh.

How I wished my mates were with me. Next time I went to town, I'd get some writing paper and write some letters. It seemed ages since I'd heard from anyone. My only contact with the mission had been about two weeks previously, when she mentioned that the priest from the mission wrote to ask her how I was progressing. "Great news," I thought. I could imagine the reply back from her, probably a real thriller!

Suddenly I heard her yoohooing out for me. I put my thoughts to one side and ran into the dining room to see what she wanted.

Over the months that I had been here, through her manner of expectation and through fear of being scolded, I had developed a habit of running whenever she needed me. So I ran in to see what she wanted.

She just told me she was on her way out and my last instructions were not to touch the phone, and also her bedroom needed doing. She told me I was to cook tea for them and have everything ready for them when they pulled up. She told me where I would find a leg of silverside. I was to boil that up and they would have it with cauliflower, pumpkin, and mashed potatoes.

So off she went with Mr. Bigelow to her car. I waited back in the dining room till I saw the car go down the driveway and head in the direction of town. I thought to myself that I'd clear all the dishes away and make sure the dining room was tidy and clean for her sons.

I wished they would hurry up and have their breakfast and go, as I felt uncomfortable knowing that they were around. I couldn't relax. I wanted to eat my bacon and eggs in peace, have my shower, and then escape down to the orchard.

The Shower

I thought I'd carry on with my usual domestic chores. I wouldn't eat anything till the sons went, and then they wouldn't be able to pimp on me—not that I knew they would, but I couldn't be sure.

So I plodded on working, and when all the silver and brassware were polished, I got stuck into cleaning out the fireplace. They had not had a fire alight the previous night, but my job was to make sure it was clean, waxed, and polished inside and all around.

When that was completed and all the dining room was spick-and-span, smelling clean and fresh with the aroma of wax and the flowers freshly picked from her garden, I closed the doors and went into the kitchen. The time was nine o'clock. Gee, I wished those boys would hurry up, because I wanted to start on the bedrooms, as time was getting on.

I thought that I'd get on with their parents' bedroom; then at least it would be all nice and clean when I was ready for my shower. So I went up the passage till I reached her bedroom.

I thought that I'd bide my time and just sort of linger on there for a while till the boys were up, because everything else was done.

I made a few trips purposely to the laundry with sheets and towels but only to check if they were up, as I had to walk past their rooms on the way out to the laundry. Every now and then a couple of doors would bang, and I'd run up the passage quick-way, just in case they came out. I was making sure I was seen working hard.

Still no sign of the boys, so I opened the back door of her bedroom which led me out into what she called the Layout Room. It was more like a verandah, only it was all closed in with fly-wire. There were potted plants set around the room to make it like outdoors. The green-foliage look was quite artistic. There was no carpet on the floor, as it was not needed, the boards being all waxed and polished. There were old wicker chairs all around the room, and a couple of rockers were placed in corners at the far end.

In the middle of this room was a sewing machine. She used to explain to me that this was where she spent most of her time when her four kids were little. As I gazed towards the sewing machine, I tried to picture her sitting there sewing, but it was hard to imagine. All I could see was someone like me hard at it on the pedal, going flat out with piles of sewing and mending to do!

I didn't mind cleaning this room. It reminded me of a museum, as all the furniture and articles were ancient or obsolete. I loved rummaging through the cupboards, looking at her odds and ends and old lace dresses, which belonged to her grandmother. I used to put some of the dresses on, and picture myself in some far-off land, living in a castle. I would get really carried away in my thoughts when I came into that room.

Finally I dragged myself away, wandered back through her bedroom door and out into the passage, when I heard some movement in the kitchen. I thought, "Oh, that's good. The two boys must be up." I heard them talking in the kitchen and went in thinking I'd better get their breakfast ready.

As soon as I opened up the kitchen door, I smelt bacon and eggs cooking. They saw me and told me that they were getting their own breakfast and not to worry about dinner for them, as they would not be back till very late. They would see their parents in town and let them know.

I shut the door behind me and left them to it, feeling pleased that I didn't have to get their breakfast. I didn't fancy pottering around in their presence. I would have felt very shamed if I'd done something silly, like dropping the teapot or spilling the sugar pot, which no doubt I would have, as I wouldn't be able to concentrate with them hanging around looking at everything I did.

By the time they had finished eating, I had both of their rooms clean, so while they were getting ready for town, I went outside to hand water the front gardens. From there I would see them drive off down the road and towards town. I didn't have to wait long. I heard their car start up, then reverse out of the garage.

I was all alone again. Off I went to the cleaning cupboard. Out with the tin of Bon Ami and the scrubbing brush—to go and do the job I had saved up. I used to hate scrubbing her shower recess, because every line between the tiles had to be scoured and polished!

Quietly I entered the bedroom, which I must say was absolutely beautiful, decorated out with pale-pink wallpaper in flower patterns. The curtains were a deep-pink colour that blended in with her lovely fluffy white carpet.

I never minded cleaning down her dressing table, as I used to love picking up her figure ornaments and her bird-shaped ones, and just gazing at them. They looked so real, with the reds, greens, and blues splashed over them.

And smelling all the different-shaped bottles of perfume! Some were so strong, I just about passed out with the whiff of them.

I put the Bon Ami down on the floor of her shower recess. This was one morning that I wasn't going to scrub those tiles. I would get myself cleaned up instead. I trotted off to her linen cupboard and picked out her best fluffy pink towels, with the aroma of lavender through them, went back to her room, and laid the towels out on her big brass bed, waiting for me there.

Then I slipped my clothes off, selected one of her fine soaps, and stepped into the recess. It was my best shower since being at the farm— oh, it was a far cry from the dog house dribble I usually stood under.

That soap smelt really sweet as I rubbed it all over me, then opened up her shampoo and emptied half the bottle on my head. There were soap suds everywhere, I got so carried away.

After my shower I pranced out on her fluffy white carpet, not noticing the wet footprints I was making. At the dressing table I just about tipped over one of her bottles and splashed perfume all over me. Then I decided to sprinkle on some powder!

I finished getting dressed and looked around—I'd given myself a double cleaning job. There were splashes and powder all over the place.

The beautiful bedroom looked like a whirlwind hit it. I didn't mind. I was smelling so nice, it made me feel so good. And when she came home, I would be smelling like vinegar again, for I had plenty of work to do.

Alone for the day, I could ask my old friend to come up for lunch. It was too late for morning tea. Reaching the orchard, I cupped my hands over my mouth and sang out his name a couple of times. I heard him answering back, "Down here, lassie," so I wandered down the land nearest to the river and spotted him picking pears and oranges.

"Hi," I said to him as if I had known him

for years. He stood up and asked me how I was feeling. I told him I was on my own, as everybody had gone to town. I told him that she wanted more fruit to be picked and bottled.

He offered to help me straightaway. I thanked him and asked eagerly if he would like to come up to the house and have dinner. He said he could. I told him that I'd go and get things ready. He said he'd be there at twelve o'clock and would bring the buckets of fruit up with him on the old tractor and trailer.

Never Put Yourself Down

I felt so happy within myself that I skipped all the way back to the house. Even the mess those boys had left behind didn't dampen my spirits as I went about cleaning the kitchen and getting this particular dinner ready.

I set the table with her finest crockery, which she only used for very important guests—I felt that her workers were just as important, and after all, it was a special occasion; old Bill was a friend of mine. I was buoyant now that I had someone I could talk to and laugh with about things. It was a far cry from walking around gloomy all day.

I laid the cold meats and salad on the table as I heard the tractor stop outside. Then I went to help Bill bring in the fruit. We put it on the sink, and I directed Bill out to the old washhouse to wash his hands as I went back into the kitchen to make the tea.

Bill came in and I told him to go through to the dining room. He sat down and sang out to me, "Hey, lassie, have you got the king and queen coming for dinner?" He gave out one of his boisterous chuckles, which echoed all through the house. I took the pot of tea in to find Bill already helping himself, so I took my place at the table.

I copied her fashion and spread the serviette across my lap. I didn't want my scraps to fall on my good clothes. I laughed out aloud. What a joke! Bill must have seen the funny side too, as we both went into fits of laughter.

Was it possible that a slave girl in second-hand clothes and an old handyman could sit up to a table laid with the best of crockery eating a meal fit for a queen?

Bill looked at me with his big sad blue eyes and said, "You keep laughing, lassie. That's better for you. Don't let the boss or anything get you down; I know it's hard on you because you are away from your home, and I suppose you miss all your mates."

With a twinge of my heart I told him, "I can only live on those memories now, Bill, as I don't know if I'll ever see home again." I changed the subject quickly, because talking and thinking about home always was a bit touchy for me. I was a very emotional person; I cried quite easily.

Now that we had eaten our main course, and I was enjoying my cup of tea, I suddenly thought about those buckets of fruit I had to prepare for preserving. As far as I was concerned, I was quite content sitting down and relaxing for the day.

Still, I thought I'd better make a good impression so that when she came home and saw all the jobs she had requested completed, she would have nothing to scowl about. Besides, if I worked now I could take it easy for the rest of the day. Why, I might even ask old Bill if he would like to come and hear me play a few tunes on the piano.

He sensed that I was deep in thought and said, "What's up, lassie?" I looked up and said that I didn't want to rush my cup of tea, then explained to him about the jobs she had lined up for me.

His wrinkled old hands still clasped around the cup, his melancholy eyes gazed up at me as he said, "Shoosh, lassie, while you are getting the fruit ready, I'll go out to the shed and chop the wood and stack the wood boxes for you." He said I didn't need to show him where to find the shed and axe, as he was an old hand at the job, and that it used to be one of his tasks when she didn't have a girl working for her.

I thanked him and said it was very kind of him. Bill said he'd have another cup of tea, so I hopped up gladly and went to make a fresh pot. When I returned, I sat down and poured his cup, then asked him if he liked music.

A big smile spread across his face. He leaned his frame into the back of his chair and said, "I sure do." He let out a bit of a chuckle, and I noticed a sparkle in his watery eyes.

"Oh, it's been a long time since I sat around the old piano. When I was a little boy back home, mother used to play in the comfort of our lounge, with an open fire spreading warmth from the hearth to every corner of the room. We used to feel so cosy as we sang to our hearts' delight—but that was a long time ago, lassie!''

We both had tender memories of childhood, but I never asked him where his home was or where he was from. I guessed in time he'd let me know. He sat there with a faraway look in his eyes. I interrupted his thoughts when I asked him if he knew songs like ''Do You Ken John Peel?'' and ''Waltzing Matilda.''

We both sat back and laughed, then stood up from the table. Bill said he'd go and get the wood chopping done; I said I'd go and get the fruit done—then we could sit back for the rest of the afternoon and entertain ourselves at the piano.

I attended to my jobs, feeling very glad that I had met someone like Bill. I didn't know how I would cope without him. He was making me see another side of life, and by thinking differently, I was becoming more bold in my attitude towards the boss.

If she scolded me or talked to me in a way where I felt like I was dirt, I sort of found courage to answer back in a way that would make her feel stupid, which I'd never dreamed of doing before to anyone, as I had a very strict upbringing. I still remember plenty of floggings I used to get at the mission for answering back to the nuns.

While I was peeling the fruit and cutting it

up, Bill came in and out with armloads of wood. I dropped what I was doing and rushed to his aid, to see if he wanted any help, as I had a guilty feeling seeing him coming and going. He kindly told me to get my fruit job done, as he couldn't wait to get to the piano. And I thought that I was the eager one . . . !

By the time Bill came in to let me know that he'd finished chopping the wood and stacking the boxes, I had all the fruit peeled and cut up and all the jars filled with sugar water. I left them standing on the kitchen cupboard. Bill explained to me that most of the wood was cut, and what he'd done was cleared all the stacked wood from the top so that at least you could see the rafters, and this would make it easier to get at.

He said, ''That should be enough to keep the boss happy for the time being; it will take at least a month to get through the lot.'' He went on to explain that he would come again to give me a hand at the chopping. Then he said, ''How's the kettle going?'' I gave out a bit of a shy giggle. ''Oh,'' I said as I rushed to the sink, ''I'll put it on.''

''Shouldn't be long before it boils.'' I sat facing Bill, just knocking my knuckles on the table. He said, ''Lassie, you look so much happier, you're blooming just like the flowers you were looking at when I first came across you and startled you out of your wits.''

I asked what ''blooming'' meant, as I didn't understand. He said, ''You look pretty and full of life.'' All of a sudden, I got real shame! I buried my head in my hands as Bill got up to switch the kettle off and turn the cups over on the saucers so he could pour our tea into them when it was ready to drink.

He said: "What's up?" I got up giggling in a bashful way. As I went to the pantry to get the sugar, I shouted back at him, "Choo, I am *winyarn*, big shame!"

Bill asked what I meant by that. I told him, "That's our way of speaking in the mission if we never had the looks, or had nothing going for us. We were *winyarn*, or open."

Bill didn't see it my way at all! He sounded a bit angry when he said, "Lassie, never put yourself down."

I giggled and said, "Na, oh, I won't!"

I slumped down into my chair and gulped a mouthful of tea, feeling more shame, as half my tea went down the front of my dress.

Bill said, "My gosh, you are a nervous one, aren't you?" I told him I couldn't help it.

He said for me not to worry about what people said. I was to hold my head up and not feel shame about myself. I was good as anybody else, if not better.

I said, "Choo, that's shame!"

As Bill laughed at my last exclamation, I guess I must have sounded quite humorous to him.

Now that we both had finished drinking our tea, we cleaned up our mess and went into the visitors' room. I lifted off the pure white linen cloth she had draped over the antique chairs and drew them up to the piano. Bill sat there, rubbing his two old bony hands together as his weary eyes scanned every corner. "My, lassie, isn't this a grand room?"

"Yes, Bill," I sighed, wishing my bedroom was as beautiful as this; but I knew this could never be.

As I ran my fingers over the piano keys, I felt real glad that I had some company. It was so much more fun! Before, when I used to come in here on my own when she went into town, I had never felt as glad as this.

It was more human having someone to answer you back than you answering only yourself back. I found I was getting into that habit since I'd been working for this boss.

Bill startled me out of my thoughts when he began clearing his throat. He asked if I knew a song called "Little Brown Jug." He started to hum the tune to see if I could recognize it.

"Oh, of course I know the song, Bill." And I started to play it straightaway, not waiting for Bill to sing. When I played one verse, I looked at him to see if he was ready to sing. I kept right on playing.

He had his mouth wide open in lockjaw fashion, but no sound was coming out. I just let it rip!

The old man looked so astonished. He peered up to the ceiling with his hands outstretched and cried out, "Where's it gone?"

I could not stop myself from laughing at him

and apologizing at the same time. In the end the old man was cracking up himself and wiping the tears from his eyes. I think that both of us were suffering with a bad case of nerves.

After we had a few more songs and laughs, our nerves settled down and our voices began to come loud and clear. Then I said to Bill, "I'll play you one of my favourite songs, one I learnt in the mission. It goes, 'I love to go a'wandering, along the mountain track . . .' "

After I finished, Bill gave me a clap. I felt very honoured, stood up, and curtsied to my one-man audience as I accepted his appreciation, then laughed as I could see the funny side of it all. If the boss knew that we had turned her V.I.P. room into a concert hall while she was in town on business—I shuddered to think what would happen. . . .

We spent the rest of the afternoon just singing and enjoying ourselves. Bill had a couple of goes on the piano. I must say he didn't do too bad. Then I asked him what the time was. He said it was four o'clock! I said, "Gee, doesn't time fly when you are having fun?" I asked Bill if he would like another cup of tea.

He was only too pleased. He jumped up and offered to put the kettle on for me and get our cups ready. I said, "There's fruitcake in the pantry on the top shelf, if you want something to eat. I would like some too."

While Bill was in the kitchen, I was making sure everything was back to normal in the V.I.P. room. I cleaned off any trace of finger marks left on her piano that might have aroused her suspicions. Now it all looked spick-and-span again, so I went out to join him in the kitchen.

Bill had the teas poured out. I took a sip of mine, then sat back in the chair. "Oh, this is just what we needed after all that singing. What do you reckon, Bill?" He said, "Sure is, lassie." Then we both helped ourselves to the fruitcake.

He said the cake tasted wonderful, and asked me if the boss baked them herself. I said, "I can't see her slaving over a hot stove. I think I heard her say that one of her friends or her daughter, Janet, the one that lives in town, bakes them."

Bill said, "We don't mind who bakes them, hey, lassie, as they taste all right to us!" We both sat back and had a good laugh. He asked if there was anything he could do to help me, as he had finished his work in the orchard and still had a spare hour up his sleeve.

I thanked him and said, "The eggs need to be collected and the gardens need watering. Other than that, everything that has to be done is done. Thanks to you, Bill. The jars of fruit are all filled on the shelf and the wood boxes are stacked up with wood. All I have to do for the meal is prepare the vegies. Before we went into the lounge to sing, I put the leg of silver-side into the pot to boil. It should be just about done by now."

"Righto, lassie, I'll go and get the eggs for

you and water the garden.'' I couldn't thank him enough. As he went out the door, I handed him the egg bucket and continued on, setting the table. I made sure the serviette rings were polished, as she had given me a scolding the day before, saying that I didn't clean them, as she could not see her face in them.

While I was just putting the finishing touches to the table, old Bill came in and asked if there was anything else he could do for me, as he had finished watering the garden. I said, ''Thanks, but everything is done.''

He looked out through the lounge window and remarked, ''Gosh, lassie, the boss is coming!''

He made a quick dash out the back as I shouted, ''See you later!'' I heard the back door slam and casually walked back into the kitchen, pottering around as I waited anxiously for her.

When the front door opened up, it was to her normal manner of speaking, ''Oh, there you are. Go out to the car and bring the stores in, and put my shopping on my bed. Did you do all your jobs today?''

I said, ''Yes, Mrs. Bigelow.''

Having had Bill around all day talking and laughing made me more confident. I wasn't feeling so withdrawn in myself anymore and must have shocked her by asking if she had a nice day in town. As expected, I was looked at in a most disdainful manner.

I went out the door to collect the shopping. When I came back inside, she was nowhere to be seen, so I put all the groceries away. Thinking she was in her room, I didn't want to go there, as the further I was away from her the better it was for me.

After the evening meal, she came out to me in the kitchen. I stopped sweeping the floor and looked her straight in her face—something I had not done since beginning to work for her. All my work was done and she could really have nothing to complain about.

She was taken aback. I noticed her flinch a bit as she commenced explaining to me that, seeing I had completed all my jobs, she was taking me into town with her tomorrow, which was Thursday.

Wondering in my mind why the sudden change, since my town day was Friday, I kept looking at her as she went on. I would have to do my morning jobs, then go and have a shower and put my working clothes on. After breakfast we would be leaving for town. "Is that understood?"

I said, "Yes, Mrs. Bigelow."

She went out, closing the door behind her. I poked my tongue out at her back; then I felt terrible and said a prayer to God, asking Him to forgive me.

As I explained before, my upbringing was strict, and if you poked your tongue at someone, that was what was called a sin, and the nuns would punish us with a hit if they caught us.

Now that I'd said my prayer, I felt better. I

put the broom away and went off to my room, never giving town another thought, as I felt pleased inside. I was going to town and that was enough—I'd be able to see my friend, the lady at the corner shop.

The Daughter's House

I fell asleep only to be awoken by the shrill ringing of the alarm clock. I turned over and groaned, thinking I could stay in my bed for a week.

As I lay flat on my back for a minute to get my brains ticking, it suddenly dawned on me that she was taking me to town. I quickly jumped out of bed, had a wash, got into my working clothes, just skimped through my jobs, then went inside to prepare breakfast.

She came in just as I had finished cooking it, and told me to get the boys' breakfast ready too, as they were also going to town and would be joining their parents at the table.

Seeing hers and her husband's ready, she took the plates of food in. As soon as I had cooked the boys' breakfast, I was to knock on the door and bring it in also. They would be waiting. So I hurried up and made the toast. By that time the bacon and eggs were sizzling, so I served everything out on their plates, put them on the trolley, and knocked on the door. She called out to come in.

The boys were there as I pushed the trolley in. As usual, everything was quiet. All eyes were on me. Suddenly the phone rang. To my surprise she turned to me and told me to answer it. As I said before, I had never used a phone, so I went over feeling very nervous and shy. Everyone was looking at me. I picked the phone up off the hook and said, "Yeah!" I could not hear anything, except a lot of noise from the other end.

She slammed her knife and fork down on the table and came rushing over to me, snatched the phone out of my hand, and pushed me out of the way. Never had a girl working for her been so stupid and humiliated her so much! She wondered whether I had any sense at all.

Holding her hand over the phone, she pointed out to me that I must speak into the speaking part, not the listening part; then she ushered me out of the room.

As I went back and sat down to eat my weeties, I wondered why I had heard someone talking at the other end of the phone.

When I finished those weeties, I thought I'd go out to the toilet, as I was still feeling a bit shaky from her sudden outburst. Just as I was ready to open the door to go out the back, she rang the bell. I made out I never heard it, snuck out quietly, and ran flat out to my own toilet. I just made it.

When I got back to the kitchen, she was standing there fuming. She shouted at me, "Where have you been?" She had given me strict orders never to leave the kitchen while her family was still in the dining room.

I apologized and told her where I had been. ''Next time you want to go to the toilet, come and let me know—and did you wash your hands after?''

I said, ''Yes,'' and she told me to get a move on, as she wasn't very happy with me or my attitude towards her; and when everything was done, I was to comb my hair and put clean working clothes on, then meet her outside near her car. With that she strutted out the door.

I sat down on the chair to collect myself again. I felt like having a good cry, but I soon rose up, wiped my eyes, and got stuck into my work.

After I completed everything, I went out, washed myself, put a clean change of clothes on, and wondered—why working clothes? Then I tripped out to her car, which was standing in the driveway.

She wasn't there, so I tried opening the doors, only to find everything locked up. So I waited patiently.

It was a couple of minutes before she came out. She opened her door and gave me her keys to open the back door. I did so, climbed in, then handed the keys to her. We were on our way.

Despite the hurt I was feeling inside, I felt glad to be going to town, although Mrs. Bigelow was as usual quiet in the car.

Soon as we reached the outskirts of Ridgeway, she veered off in an unexpected direction. I saw a sign saying HOSPITAL, and I was thinking, ''That's funny—we're not going to the shops,'' when she turned to the left and stopped outside this beautiful home. The gardens were so colourful. Every flower seemed to be in bloom.

I noticed that the house was built high up. And from here I could see all the township as I looked back over my shoulder. I was still sitting in the car waiting for her as she made her way up the garden path.

A couple of kids ran out to her, singing out ''Nanna!'' as they grabbed one of her hands on either side and walked with her. It was then that I realized this was her daughter's house. The one that came to see her every now and again.

Then her daughter, Janet, came out to greet her. They stood talking for a while. I wished that she would hurry up, as I wanted to go to the shops! I felt hot in the car and could have done with a bottle of cool drink.

In the meantime, while they were still talking, her grand-kids were coming down, peeping into the car at me, then running away laughing and sniggering. I felt like a monkey in a cage.

Then I saw them both coming down the path. When they reached the car, she told me to get out and follow her up to the house. I was beginning to get confused, and wondered whether I would go into town at all.

When I reached the house, her daughter asked me inside. It was beautiful, just like her mum's. Then she came over to me with a list

of duties to be done. I looked at it, then at her,
and it suddenly dawned on me why I'd been
brought to town a day early.

Mrs. Bigelow explained to me, in front of her
daughter, that every fortnight she was bringing
me in to clean Janet's house while they both
went shopping.

With those instructions she left me. Janet
called for her kids, and they all trooped outside,
climbed into their car, and drove off.

I sat down on the chair in her kitchen. As I
went through the list of jobs her daughter had
given, I felt very downhearted. The chores
weren't anything new. They were just what I
did for her mum; but where to start, where to
begin? The whole house was a mess!

I began with the kids' bedroom. There were
clothes everywhere. It took me nearly two hours
to get through the room. I wondered whether I
would finish the rest of the house before they
got back. I looked at the time. It was twelve
o'clock.

I went and looked in her fridge. There was a
jam sandwich on a tin plate. I presumed she
had left that for my lunch. I didn't feel like a
jam sandwich, so I helped myself to cold meat
and salad, then I went down to her backyard to
see if she had chooks. She did.

Screwing the sandwich up, I chucked it to
them. They were quite pleased to get it too, as
they scrambled over one another for every bit
of bread.

Feeling worn out, I went back into the house

to continue on with my work. It was nearly half past three by the time I had finished cleaning. The whole house smelt fresh and clean, as I had used plenty of Dettol to freshen the place up. I looked around the house and felt something was missing.

"Oh, yes, that's it. I'll go and pick some flowers and put them around the rooms."

So I went to find some vases, which she kept in the laundry—put them on the shelf in the kitchen, then got some scissors out of the drawer, and went outside. I cast my eyes over her beautiful garden, then went over and snipped some red, pink, and white carnations. I held them to my nose. "Mm, they are beautiful"—and I breathed in deeply the fragrance.

I added a few other types of flowers, snapdragons, hollyhocks. Now that I had bunched up a variety of flowers in my hand, I went back into the kitchen to place them in the vases and arrange them around the house.

I felt pleased with myself, as the flowers made the rooms so much more alive, and I thought I'd take myself off on a bit of a walk, seeing I had done my jobs. I strolled down the garden path, casually taking in the scenery all around me. It sure was a pretty town. The green hills towering behind the houses reminded me of those around Wandering Mission.

While I stood there gazing around, I had the feeling I was begin watched. I looked to my left and right and saw a couple of ladies out in their front garden talking together and pointing at me. When I looked over the road the same thing was happening. There were ladies everywhere over the fences in the front yards—all eyes were on me!

Being used to talking to old Bill, my shyness having worn off me, I thought I'd better go over and ask the ladies if something was wrong. I made my way over to the nearest house, and when I got to the fence, glanced up. There was no one in sight. I sang out, "Are you there?"

Then I caught a glimpse of someone peering out from a window. They reminded me of a mob of chooks in a cage.

I went back inside the daughter's house and had just sat myself down comfortably on a chair in her lounge when I heard a car door slam. I quickly got up, ran to the kitchen, and made out I was busy wiping the sink.

When the door opened, her two grandchildren came in, laughing and sniggering. They said, "Nanna wants you!"

I left them there laughing as I went out the door. As soon as the boss saw me, she told me to hurry up and take the shopping in, since she had to take me back to the farm to get tea on for the family.

Janet hardly ever spoke to me on those fortnightly working days in town. The only time she smiled was when I caught her off guard and she had no choice. It was only when I looked after her kids that she had to face me, to tell me what times to send the boys in for their washes or meals.

Mrs. Bigelow and her daughter walked past me as I quickly began unloading the shopping, took it into the house, and put everything away. By then she was saying good-bye to her daughter.

She told me to get into the car! As we made our way back, I had a notion she was going to tell me something.

Sunday Best

Back at my normal place of work, as I set about doing my chores, I tried not to get myself all worked up about whether it was to be good news or bad. I knew that I had to accept it, because in those days we had no choice. We just had to take what came along.

Later, having cleaned up after tea, I was sweeping the floor, and sure enough, just as I had expected, she came in. She told me that, seeing I had been there eight months and had done such a good job—I nearly fainted, thinking, "Wonders will never cease"—she had a surprise. She explained that a friend of hers had hired a girl from the same mission to work for her on their farm on which they bred racehorses.

I had never heard of racehorses and didn't understand what she meant. Naturally, I thought she meant horses running up and down the paddock, and that was why she called them racehorses.

Well, she continued on, the friend was arriving at their farm tomorrow and had asked if she could bring this girl into town in a fortnight's time to meet me, which I thought was quite humane of her friend.

"So, I won't be taking you into town with me on Thursday, which would have been your town day. You can wait till next Friday, when my friend will bring the mission girl in."

As much as I hated my boss, I could have hugged her for joy. I couldn't control my emotions. My tears splashed onto the floor. It seemed like years since I had seen anyone from home.

I was dying to ask her: What was the girl's name? She just told me to wipe my eyes, as I was a big girl and only babies carried on that way.

Over the months that I had been there I had written a couple of letters to the mission, but never received an answer. Now I'd find out from this girl all the news. She'd tell me everything! Oh, I was so overwhelmed with joy inside me that nothing else mattered. I put the broom away, went to my bedroom, knelt down, and thanked God for letting me be near my mate.

Next day when she went into town as usual, I was still bubbling with joy. As soon as everyone left the farm and I was on my own, I couldn't wait to run flat out down to the orchard to tell old Bill the good news!

He felt very pleased and happy for me. He wiped his eyes and said, "Hey, lassie, I can see a change in you already."

I told him I couldn't wait to see her.

He asked me where was I the other day? I told him, "She took me into town to clean her daughter's house out. She's taking me in every second Thursday to do her daughter's cleaning."

He scratched his old head and said, "By gosh, some people have got it easy!" I didn't understand what he meant by that. Then he said, "Let's go on up to the house and have a cup of tea. I fancy a bit of fruitcake, too," and he gave a chuckle.

The fortnight went by quickly, and then came the day I was meeting my friend from back home. I was so anxious to find out who she was, I took extra care in getting ready for town. I put on one of my Sunday best dresses, a beautiful pink one which reached down to my ankles; stockings; corset; my one-and-only best pair of sandals; and a bright-green scarf, which I carefully tied around my head. I got my old purse and stuffed it down my bra.

With a feeling of importance I walked out of my room and down the driveway, to where Mrs. Bigelow had the car parked.

When she came out, I was standing proudly beside it. She sort of brushed past and remarked to me she'd let me know when there was a circus in town, as maybe they'd have an act in the show for me. She told me to open up my door and get in. Then she started up the car, and away we went into town.

I had butterflies all the way. When we got to the bus stop, I saw them standing there. Soon as she stopped the car, I started giggling, with my hands over my mouth. It was Anne! We used to fight like cats and dogs all the time at the mission. She called me Sprattie and I called her Horsey.

I climbed out, and we both stood waiting by our cars until our employers finished talking. Then they turned to us and told us they would pick us up here in about an hour's time. They strutted off down the street like a pair of chooks on their high heels.

We both laughed out loud then said, "Hello." We were so glad to see one another, we became the best of mates. I asked her how everyone was.

She said, "Good!" The nuns were okay, and a few girls had received my letters; but the priest had read them and he didn't like what I wrote. I never received any answer.

I was feeling too happy to be upset about the priest in the mission. I told her to come and meet my friend at the corner shop, and I'd buy an ice cream for her.

We both linked arms and made our way down to the shop, laughing and giggling about old times at Wandering.

When we reached the shop, I pushed Horsey up to the counter to introduce her to my friend. She said, "Hello, dear. I bet you're glad you met up with a mate."

I told my friend at the shop, "Anne grew up with me in the mission—we were in the same class."

She grabbed Horsey's hand and said that it was very nice to meet her, then told us to sit down and make ourselves at home.

I ordered two milk shakes, two chocolates, and some lollies and biscuits for us. As we sat and drank our milk shakes, Anne said that the lady in the shop was different from the one she worked for.

She asked me how the missus I was working for treated me. I told her it was a beautiful place; but that the people were funny. They didn't talk to me at all, and all I seemed to be doing was working, and when I did try to talk to her, she didn't answer or even look at me.

Then she asked me did I get wild?

I said I couldn't get wild, because they were white people and our bosses. What could we do? Nothing! I even had to clean her daughter Janet's house.

Anne asked me if the daughter was pretty? I looked at her in surprise and said she was a "pretty kid." We both had a good laugh.

I explained to her about sleeping in the garage, and we compared different things, the places we slept and ate and washed in—even our toilet rooms. My mate told me she had to walk a mile past the horse stables to reach hers. We both saw the funny side and killed ourselves laughing. I told her about the phone incident, and she cracked up again.

All too soon it was time to go back to the

bus stop to wait for our bosses to pick us up and take us back to their farms. We both said we'd see one another again in the next fortnight.

Going Home

Two months before Christmas, Mrs. Bigelow again came to me while I was out working one morning in the garden. This particular day was a Tuesday. She caught me unawares. She didn't tell me she had anything important to say; she just stood there and came out with it, as I was tidying the lawn. I could go home to the mission for two weeks' holiday. Starting the very next day.

I nearly buckled at the knees; I didn't know what to do or say to her. She went on. "Have your things packed tonight and I will drive you into the bus stop, where you can catch the bus which will take you to Bunbury. Then you can catch a train to Armadale, and the priest will be there to pick you up and drive you on to the mission."

And off she strutted back into the house, leaving me standing there dumbfounded at the suddenness of it. My feelings were mixed. Shocked and dazed, I finished my weeding and sneaked into my bedroom, out in the old garage.

There I sat on my bed to let the good news of going home sink into my head. I dragged my case out from under the bed, got my towel, and with a quick striking action dusted it off. I began to be so overwhelmed with joy at going home that I cried as I started packing my case. The tears of relief were dropping onto all my clothes, but I couldn't care less; nothing mattered now.

In this way I was so engrossed in my packing that I never heard my bedroom door open. I nearly dropped the case back on the floor as she startled me out of my wits.

"How dare you come in here and start packing your clothes! Just because I said you could go home for holidays doesn't mean you have to stop work." I didn't know what to say.

"I want all your jobs finished for the day. I told you to pack your case tonight, which will be after nine by the way you are going. Now drop what you are doing and get out of here and do your work. Otherwise you won't be going at all. I shall ring up the priest and cancel your ticket.

"By the way, can't you clean this room up? It smells horrible. It looks like a rubbish dump. Cobwebs on the wall, dirty windows . . . and clear this dust away . . ." She slammed the door as she went, and I rushed to the toilet for refuge.

For the rest of the day I tried not to be upset by her sudden outburst. I kept thinking of the mission I would soon see, the nuns, and my mates, and that got me through, until late that night I just about fell into my room and faced the packing. I just gathered all my stuff up and chucked everything in the case.

I thought I was tired, yet I sat up on my bed for most of the night. The excitement was growing deeper. I fell into a restless sleep.

When daylight came I took my big brown suitcase and carried it into the kitchen and laid it on the floor. So pleased to have everything packed, I thought I'd have my breakfast early. So I was having a feed of weeties when she stubbed her foot on my case.

She was furious. "What's this thing doing here right in front of my dining room door? I nearly broke my leg." I jumped up and apologized. "Take that case right outside this very minute, and then you can set about getting my breakfast ready. All your jobs have to be done before we can leave for town." So I hurried to finish my weeties.

I set about the work, mumbling at her under my breath. I was feeling real glad that I was leaving her, at least for a while. When it was time to go to the bus stop, she had the car ready in the driveway. I went to my room to pick up my scarf, and shut the door on the cobwebs and dust. I put my old brown case in the boot, took my place in the backseat of her car, and then we were away.

When we arrived at the station there were people everywhere and a big green-and-pale-yellow bus was already waiting. I didn't know anything about getting on buses, as this was the first time I'd ever caught one.

Without looking at me, she passed me her keys to open the boot. When I had taken my case out, Mrs. Bigelow told me flatly to go up to the man in the office—he would help me. With that she left me standing there and drove off.

Nervously I walked up to the bus and stood there. I put the scarf on my head, although it was not cold or windy. I found myself brushing the pleats of my long skirt—it reached my ankles—and straightened my white blouse. I noticed the green embroidery around the edges, looked at my yellow shoes, which had seen better days. And just as I picked my case up to carry it aboard the bus, I was tapped on the shoulder.

I turned to see a gentleman in uniform grey trousers and a neat shirt and tie. "Where are you going to, madam?" he asked me, businesslike but friendly. I was so excited, I told him. "Home to Wandering Mission!"

People on the bus were having a good gander at me. I looked up to the windows, smiled at them, and got a few smiles back. The man in the uniform asked me if I had a ticket. All I could tell him was that I had a case and needed some help on the bus with it. He asked if I had some money. When I told him yes, he said, "Well, give me your case. I'll take it and put it in the storage compartment at the back of the bus. You go and sit down, and when you hear a feller asking if everyone has their tickets, you tell him you haven't got one.''

I thanked him and climbed on the bus to join all those curious people, and sat down beside this old lady, who nodded to me as I said hello, still feeling nervous. I was just relaxing when the bus started up.

Another gentleman in uniform came down the aisle with a punch in his hand, calling out for tickets. I jumped up and said, ''I haven't got one, sir.'' I heard giggles everywhere as the man came over to me, offering a little piece of paper. I took the ticket from him and sat back. He just stood there next to me in the aisle, waiting.

The old lady beside me leaned over and whispered, ''You have to pay five pounds, dear.'' I quickly fumbled in my old brown bag, which had no zip pocket. All my money was lying loosely at the bottom. I raked amongst the lollies and hair clips and other odds and ends and finally pulled out a five-pound note. I gave that to the uniformed man, who turned out to be the driver. He went away down the aisle scratching his head. The people were all staring at me again, so I gave them another smile!

I sat back in my seat as the bus drove out of the station. The little old lady asked if I wanted a magazine to read. I said thanks and took it from her but I did not really want to read and just skipped through the pages—I felt tired suddenly and handed it back. She said, ''You're going home, hey?''

I told her all about myself—where I worked, where I came from, what I did. I noticed the passengers glancing my way. Her voice croaked, "I'll bet you can't wait to see your friends." I giggled and wriggled on the seat, looked out the window, and wished that the bus would hurry up. She said it wouldn't be long now. She was going to Perth to visit relations.

The bus stopped in different towns all the way along and picked up passengers, and I dozed off to sleep. I woke with the old lady tugging at my sleeve. The bus was in Bunbury. I sat up, rubbed my eyes, and heard the bus conductor telling us to collect our cases, go into the front office, and fix up our tickets to board the train for Perth. We had an hour in Bunbury for lunch.

The town was huge compared to Ridgeway, bigger shops, more people and cars going everywhere. Although I was hungry, I was too scared to cross the street. I felt safer where I was standing.

The old lady from the bus hobbled up to me and asked if I knew where to go. I told her that I didn't know where to go or what to do. She took me by the hand and told me not to be scared, she'd look after me. She shuffled along beside me to the office and they stamped my ticket for Armadale, where Father would pick me up.

I started to feel pleased and proud, and to have butterflies, knowing that in a couple of hours' time I'd be home again. The man told us everything would be fixed up about our cases; the lady took my ticket from him and passed it to me. I was so pleased that this old lady bothered to help at all.

She asked if I was hungry—I was starving. We went to the station cafe, where there were people lined up in a queue waiting for service. She told me to go and sit down and wait till she came with refreshments. The cafe was packed and I pushed my way past people to an empty table.

As I sat there waiting for my elderly friend, I felt strange somehow. It just didn't seem right, me sitting there with all these people and this white lady helping me. Being stuck with Mrs. Bigelow for so long I just wasn't used to it. Here it felt so different, people happy, watching one another eat.

Then the little lady turned up with a woman in a white apron, carrying teacups and two rounds of sandwiches. I was told not to be shy as she passed me a cup and saucer. I ate and left the crumbs without bothering to tidy up, as I would have at Mrs. Bigelow's kitchen table. ''You must have been hungry,'' the old lady said. Half a sandwich had satisfied her.

The waitress in a white apron collected our dishes and put a slip of paper in front of us. My friend explained that I had to pay five shillings. So I fumbled in my bag once again and handed the money over.

On the platform people were pushing and shoving. I hung on to my friend, scared I might lose her in the crowd. We boarded the train and walked up and down like lost sheep until we found our compartment. I discovered you had your own seat numbered on the ticket and couldn't just sit anywhere.

We settled down and I thanked my friend for being so kind—I felt like crying, but she told me not to worry. She rested her hand gently on mine. I must have looked real lost and in need of someone. After all, I was only a kid.

When she took her hand off mine, I could feel a big lump forming in my throat and put my head down. I was choked with emotion and mixed feelings. I thought, "Why can't old Bigelow be kind and helpful?" And I shuddered at the thought of going back to her.

The old lady asked me if I was all right. "Yes," I lied. All round us the passengers were seated in the compartment; the train engine started with a roar and a whistle. I nearly jumped out of my seat, as this was my first experience of trains. My friend kept reassuring me, but I still found it scary. She said if I felt nervous, it would help if I went to sleep.

So I put my head back and dozed, still shaky. Time must have passed, because I was startled out of a nap as the train whistled and roared into a small station. The little old lady leaned over to me. "This is your stop." She clasped my hand in hers. We were at Armadale.

She wished me luck. I started to tremble and felt weak at the knees as I glanced out the window. I saw Brother Leonard and my tears started to fall uncontrollably.

Billy Boy

As I walked behind the people to get out of the carriage, I wiped my face on the inside of my skirt. Then Brother came over to me and gave me a hug. I took my scarf off, put my head down, and scraped the dirt with my foot. His arm still over my shoulder, he said, "How are you, Billy Boy?" That was one of my nicknames in the mission.

Still feeling shy but relieved that my journey was over and seeing Brother Leonard again, I couldn't have been more happy. I knew I'd soon be home. As kids we used to think Brother Leonard funny, with a round face and short build, a big belly, and braces to hold his pants up.

He also smoked a big pipe, and when he used to play games with us, like kicking a ball round the field, he looked so funny running around that we rolled over laughing.

Brother turned to me and said, "Come on, Billy Boy, we'll go and get your case." So I followed him to the luggage place and then walked over to the utility he had parked a short distance from the station.

Brother opened up the front door of the ute, and as I sat in it, I glanced back at the station. I had a sickly feeling inside me, knowing that the same train would be taking me back.

As we drove away, Brother Leonard asked me how I was getting on. Did I miss them at the mission? "Yes!" I replied. "And how are the people you work for?" "All right," I said.

In those days, not so long ago either, we were not allowed to say anything against our white bosses. So I hid my feelings and told him they were good and I liked it there, just to please him. If only he had known how I felt.

Then, as we got going further down the track, Brother filled me in on all the news. The head priest had bought a brand-new bus to take the kids out to different towns for school sports and outings. He'd done away with the old cattle truck we once travelled in. He'd also purchased a couple of new cars, and this was one of them.

Some of the girls who'd been little in my time were still there, as working girls. Others had returned to their families, as their mums and dads found out where they had gone to and came to take them back to their real homes. I knew my own dad wasn't alive, but I still wondered how my mother must be doing, up there in Geraldton. I had learnt that she lived in Geraldton. She once came down to Wandering and tried to visit, but I had not been allowed to see her.

"Of course, you know Anne left to work near where you are staying." He sounded pleased. I said, "Yes, I was glad to see her in town; she gave me all the news about the old place." Brother asked me how she was coping. I told him, "Good," and that the people drove us in from our farms on a Friday afternoon to meet one another in town. He thought that was very generous of them.

I relaxed as Brother drove on, and we yarned about the good old days. Soon we were at the mission turnoff, which was marked by a sign saying, *To St. Francis Xavier Native Mission,* WANDERING BROOK. Brother slapped his hand on my knee, and I jumped in fright. "Billy Boy," he said, "we'll be home soon." I wriggled around a bit to look out my window, feeling that lump again in my throat.

How could I have forgotten these familiar places, where as a child I roamed right through the bush? I noticed all our landmarks were still there, and I thought they would never change. We passed a big crucifix out in the bush. I think one of the brothers built that statue, which was about five miles from the mission. It stood there for years.

We used to walk to that crucifix, and it had seemed so far. When we reached it, we used to climb up and sit down on the side of it, as the cross was mounted on this wide, round stand, which gave us a lot of room to rest on. We got our breath back there and then we'd go on to a certain clump of gum trees, as the crucifix used to be a sign for our gum trees—a step on the way there.

Further down the track was a big clearing of land, where we used to pick wildflowers, smokebush, kangaroo paws. We'd come out of the clearing with the paddocks around us and the bush left behind.

Now the car passed the dams we swam in. Brother chuckled. "Remember those dams, Billy Boy?" We both laughed to think of those earlier days.

"This is it, Billy Boy, home." It was about five and still pretty light as the buildings came into view. My heart was pounding as we passed the old working shed down the hill, and the fields where we picked puddings. They were a type of grass with a long stem and a little bundle of seeds on top, which we used to eat. They were lovely.

Then we made our run up the straight road to the mission itself. Brother stopped outside the girls' dormitory—there were kids running in all directions as they crowded around, pushing and shoving. I was shy when I saw their snotty noses all pressed up to the window and their cheesy grins. I put my hand out the window to grab their hands, till the door opened up and made us let go. Just as well, as I felt like my arms were being yanked off.

There were still a lot of familiar faces in the crowd. I said hello to Father and some of the nuns. I was so glad to see them. Sister Headmaris, who had scolded me often in the kitchen, came over and shook my hand. The tears were welling up in my eyes. She said, "How are you, Glenyse? It's good to see you again," and I noticed that her eyes were glistening too.

Father came over and gave me a pat on the shoulder. I nearly keeled over. "Come, Glenyse, you must be hungry," said Sister Headmaris. And with kids all around, tugging at me, digging me in the ribs and running away, I followed Sister over to the dining room. Then I knew I was home.

It was so good to see them again, but my closest mates, the ones I went to school with, were all gone. They were making lives for themselves somewhere out in the world.

I stayed for three weeks. They didn't want me to work, but I found something to do helping in the kitchen. It was different now that I'd been out working and come back. I enjoyed being with Sister Headmaris; she was so pleased with me and proud of me, as if I was her own daughter.

It broke my heart to have to say good-bye again, because somehow I knew there was no returning for me.

As it turned out, I didn't go back by train after all. Instead a couple of young teachers from the mission gave me a lift, since they were going through to Bunbury. I just sat in their car and cried all the way. They couldn't understand why I was so unhappy, and I couldn't tell them. I was real *winyarn* at going back.

Prepared

When I arrived at Ridgeway, she was waiting by the bus stop to pick me up. I went back to playing a dummy's life again.

I found it hard within myself to get used to the place again after being surrounded by so many friends. My heart wasn't in my work. The only thing that kept my spirits up was the chance to meet Horsey, who I couldn't wait to see on that following Friday, to tell her all the news from home.

The journey into town was the same as usual, but to break the monotony, I commented to the boss about the scenery—how beautiful and fresh everything looked, the wildflowers growing on the sides of the road and the hills. She made no reply, but I did notice that she looked up.

We stopped at our usual meeting place, at an old school bus stop, and my friend was standing nearby, with her boss. They exchanged a few words, then told us we had an hour to do our business. We were to meet them back here at the cars.

Our employers trotted off. Me and Horsey

linked arms and headed for the milkbar, laughing and talking. I was so glad when I saw my mate. I told her that I had gone home. She was feeling like me, real homesick.

Although she hadn't been at the job as long as I, she was beginning to resent the place and the people she worked for. Our feelings were mutual. I told her how my holiday went and who was still there, what sisters and brothers were still there, and that I didn't want to leave to come back here again. We agreed that we couldn't stand it anymore.

Our friend, the owner of the shop, was happy to see me again and said she had missed me on those two Fridays I was due into town. When I told her I'd been back home to see all my mates, she said, ''That's nice for you. I'll bet Mrs. Bigelow missed you, though.'' I said that she must have, as I had double the workload since getting back.

Horsey and I looked out of her shop window and asked, ''How come all these coloured lights and paper were hanging off the posts in the street?'' There seemed to be a lot more people everywhere. She was surprised. ''Didn't your bosses tell you girls? There's a fair here on Saturday.''

We asked her what a fair was, as our minds were vague on that. ''It's like a fun day, where people who make cakes and jams have stalls to sell them and get prizes for the best. Plenty of merry-go-rounds, and you can win prizes too on the chocolate wheel. People travel from as far away as Busselton and Bunbury to come here with their families. It's a family day; you can have lots of fun."

Horsey just said, "Oh—I wonder if we'll be going." I grabbed my mate by the arm and pulled her towards a table. "Come on, me and you sit here and have this drink. Don't think about the fair. We'll be working flat out."

As we sat there looking at one another, a thought struck me and I asked Anne if her boss made jam, like my boss. "Yeah," she said, "why are you asking?" "Well, they might take us to help carry their stuff."

"Oh, don't talk silly," she grumbled, but I was hard to convince. I jumped up and grabbed her by the arm again. "Let's go!" Horsey Anne had a shocked look on her face, wondering what I was up to. I called out to our friend behind the counter. "See you later." She seemed astonished. "Oh, you're off already, girls?" I yelled, "Yes—we've got business to do!"

As we went out the door, I pushed Anne along, telling her to walk fast to the bank. I never answered her curious questions. At the bank I asked her, "You got your bank book with you?" It was in her handbag. I pushed her, still wondering, inside and up to the counter.

A man with a real business look about him asked if he could help us, and I eagerly told him, "Yes, we would like to get some money out; we're going to the fair." My friend gave me a dig in the ribs. The man looked at us sternly and asked in his deep voice, "How much?"

"How much have I got?" I replied, as I had no idea. He looked in our books and said I had fifty pounds and Anne forty. So I asked for forty and Horsey asked for twenty. As he went away to get our money, and people walked up and down, my friend whispered to me that we'd get into trouble for running away. I giggled and hit her on the back. "As long as our bosses make jam and cakes, we'll be going, can't you see? They'll need us to help them. You know yourself they won't carry their own stuff."

She sort of laughed and blurted, "Choo—but if we don't go, what about this money?" I reckoned we could hang on to it and spend it next shopping day. We were so busy whispering and laughing, when a deep voice brought us to attention: "Would you like to come and get your passbooks and cash?"

We stuffed it in our bags, and as we went out the doors, I said to Horsey, "At least we are prepared; we've got money. You and I could have a ride on the merry-go-round!" We went along laughing and getting excited.

While we sat on the bus stop waiting for our bosses, I told her not to give any signs away that we knew about the fair. "We'll just carry on in our normal way and do our jobs. We'll say prayers tonight. God will help us."

When the bosses turned up, I tugged at Horsey's dress and she gave me a nudge in the back, then we went to our cars and drove our separate ways back to the farms.

I crept into bed that night after my jobs feeling a little downhearted, as she had never mentioned the fair.

Baalay!

Next morning, when I came into the kitchen with a couple of oranges to squeeze for her, I had completely forgotten about the fair. She was already up and turned to me straightaway. "Oh, there you are. Look, hurry up with my juice, as we've got a very busy day. Get my bottles of jam out of the pantry and give them a wipe over. Be careful that you don't rub the labels off!

"Then pack them very neatly in my cane basket, on the bench over there. I am entering them in the Ridgeway Fair, and you are coming with me to help carry things. We will leave after breakfast. Hurry up, because I have to be there before Mr. Bigelow opens the fair."

Without showing any emotions, I went about my jobs in my usual casual way. When I got to my room, I shut the door behind me quietly. Then I jumped for joy. I chucked my work clothes up in the air and started humming and singing, as I set about getting dressed.

Taking care I looked nice for the fair, I put on a pleated white skirt, a blue blouse, a faded white pair of shoes, and a pink hair band around my head, instead of a scarf. Then I knelt down beside my bed to say thanks to God for letting me go to the fair.

I left my room like a whirlwind swept through it. She was already waiting in the car and told me to hurry up and run to the kitchen and get the basket of jams. She told me to sit with it beside me in the car and hang on to it.

At the fairground there were cars and people everywhere. I wondered if my mate was here. I followed my boss with the basket of jams like a lost lamb, still wondering if my mate was coming. Kids were running everywhere, music belting out all over the ground, swings were set up, and coloured lights were flashing on the merry-go-round.

When we reached the judging stall, all I could hear was, "Hello, Tracey, it's good to see you again. You could ask your dark servant to place the jars up on the shelf. Wish you luck." While they were all jabbering, I got busy setting the jars up and thought to myself, "All these women are a bunch of chooks." Then a voice piped up amongst the jabbering, "Oh, here comes Prue Follington."

I whirled around and saw Mrs. Follington with Horsey beside her, carrying a basket. I suddenly felt happy putting the jars up. They could joke about Mrs. Follington getting her dark servant to put jams up next to Mrs. Bigelow's. I stood and waited for Horsey to do it, while in the meantime our two bosses got talking.

They both turned to us—we could walk around, but must report back to them at dinnertime because they were leaving then to go back to their farms. We never wasted any time.

We had rides on the merry-go-round, ate our fill of fairy-floss, tried our luck on the chocolate wheel, bought ourselves some pies and drinks, and found a table and bench under a tree. While we were sitting there joking and eating, and laughing if anyone comical walked past us, we noticed another Aboriginal girl with four white kids, just walking around and looking at the game stands.

I said to Horsey, "Hey, who's that Nyoongah girl over there?" Anne didn't know her, and we decided to wait till she came a bit closer. We both sat there straining our eyes until she took hold of one of the kids' arms and walked our way. "Look out, she's coming our way," I said to Horsey. "Baalay, make out we never seen her."

So we both turned our heads and made out we had never seen her. Next minute we heard this voice. "Hello, you two." We looked surprised. Then she asked, "You're not Sprattie and Horsey?" We smiled and said yes, trying to focus this face in front of us.

She said, "Don't you know me from the mission? I'm Rae Miller." Of course we knew her. We all hugged one another, so very glad to meet up after years. How could we have missed that big forehead—we used to joke about the way it stuck out—and her plump body. We were old mission buddies. Excited, we talked and laughed. She told us she worked in Donnybrook and asked us what were we doing here.

We told her all about the people we worked for, how we hated being treated that way. She was sorry to hear it. We felt strange listening to her tell us how the white people she worked for made her one of the family. She ate with them, played with the kids, went to the pictures with them. I didn't know what to say. I changed the subject and asked her if she knew where different girls we grew up with had gone. Like us, she never heard.

Then she went on to say that on her holidays with the people she worked for, at a beautiful place called Dunsborough, near the beach, she did bump into one of the girls who used to be there with us in the mission. And her name was Kaylene. Kaylene—who had married the schoolteacher!

We were so glad to hear that news, me especially. I was always close to this girl in the mission and always wondered what had happened to her. Rae had her address and suggested I write to her. Maybe instead of going to Wandering Brook for holidays again, I could go there.

Holidays were a long way off. We kept on talking, when we suddenly realised it was twelve. We told Rae we hated to leave her but we must get back to our bosses, as we were returning to our farms to work that afternoon.

Before we departed, I reached for Rae's hands and she grabbed mine. I said, "See you in Dunsborough, mate." Then we walked back to our cars, me and Horsey. We had the same thoughts of how lucky Rae was, and wished our bosses were like that.

Before I went to sleep that night back at the Bigelow farm, I sat down and wrote my letter to Kaylene in Dunsborough.

Shearers' Lunch

So I settled back into the routine of the year at the farm, waiting for a letter from Kaylene.

Shearing was on, and it was the middle of the week. That used to be a busy time for everyone. I had to help make morning tea and lunches for the shearers. When it was time for either morning tea or lunch, Robert, her youngest son, used to come up to the house to collect the food in a basket.

From the top of the hill, where the house stood, you could view the goings-on and hear the shouting of men and the machines and baaing of lambs and ewes. The shearing sheds were about half a mile from the house.

It was a quarter to twelve and I was busy in the kitchen, putting the last lot of sandwiches in the basket, which was laden high with food. I didn't know exactly how many blokes there were, but I did overhear Robert tell his mother the other day that there were about ten men—it looked like she was going to feed an army.

The phone rang while I was cleaning up, and I heard her walk into the dining room and take the receiver off the hook. She spoke for about twenty minutes, then came into the kitchen to tell me that I was to take the lunches to the men, as they were very busy and Robert couldn't come to pick the basket up. One of the shearers was sick and couldn't make it in to work.

She said, "Drop what you're doing, take the flask of tea and the basket of sandwiches." So I grabbed it and away I went with my heavy load, humming as I went along, glad of the break—I was out of the house.

When I got outside, I thought, "Instead of walking right around the road, I'll take a short cut." I walked straight down the hill and over to the creek, which had this makeshift bridge going across it.

There were ropes on both sides and boards going straight down the middle. Water was still flowing strongly under it. When I reached the bridge, I put the basket and flask down and sat on the grass to rest my body, as it was aching through the strain of carrying that load of food.

When I felt better, I picked up the flask and sandwiches. I was in good spirits as I tiptoed onto the bridge, which was very wobbly. With one hand up clinging to the rope, I stooped down low and sort of dragged the basket to the middle. Next minute, without warning, I found myself on my backside in the water, and the sandwiches floating beside me.

I got such a shock when I felt how cold the water was, I screamed, sprang up, and ran towards the house. When I finally reached it, I banged right into Mrs. Bigelow. She was out in the garden, looking at her flowers. My heart sank. I think she got more of a shock than I when she saw the sad state of affairs I was in.

Before she could scold me, I began gibbering, as I couldn't control the knocking of my teeth, when suddenly her son Robert pulled up in the car and handed his mum the wet basket and cracked thermos. He'd found them floating down the creek when he took his dog to round up a stray sheep, and must have figured out what happened to their dinner.

She turned to me in front of her son. "You clumsy, stupid girl. Can't you do anything right? You've upset the whole shearing team now. All work has stopped because the men refuse to start again till they have something to eat. I just can't trust you to do anything—that bridge was made for ducks!

"You had to come along and wreck it. I ought to make you go down and mend it. Now get inside and get yourself cleaned up and report back to me in the kitchen when you hear me come back from the shearing shed. By that time you should be looking respectable."

I noticed the sheepish grin on her son's face as he glanced at me before following his mother back into the kitchen. I felt shame as I slipped into my room and shut the door.

End of the Road

One sunny morning in mid December I wandered down to the orchard to have a yarn to my old mate Bill and ask him up for a cup of tea and some cake.

I hadn't seen him for a few days, as Mrs. Bigelow had the flu and I was kept in the house to tend to her needs. I never had the chance to go down there for some friendly company. Now that she was better and gone into town, I was left alone as usual.

I got to the gate, cupped my hands, and yelled in my loudest voice, "Bill, I'm here, where are you?" I heard his call come back very faint from somewhere down towards the river. As I walked in that direction, I spotted his bent figure, raking up around the apricot trees.

When I reached him I noticed how pale and weak he was looking; he just didn't seem to be his normal happy self as he leaned his old frame up against an apricot tree.

He said, "Hi, lassie—where you been these last couple of days?" I was so busy jabbering away to him, glad of the fact I was out of the house; then I sort of glanced at him and the look on his old face stopped me. It made me feel he wanted to tell me something.

"What's wrong?" I asked. He answered with a faraway look on his face, "How long will you be working here, lassie?" I was very concerned now. "Bill, why are you asking me that?" He cleared his throat and in a shaky voice said he was at the end of the road. I asked him, "What road?" as I never understood what he was talking about.

Bill sort of half laughed and explained he wasn't coming to work for Mrs. Bigelow again; he was getting too sick and too old to continue. He was just going home to settle down. Before I could say anything more to him, he went on, "That's why I asked you how long you will be here. I'm going to miss you, lassie. . . ." His clear blue eyes welled up with water.

It was hard for me to tell him that I also wanted to leave—I was still afraid to tell anyone. I looked the other way and said I'd made up my mind, I was going—where I didn't know. "But I'm going," I told him, as I put my head down and drew with my foot in the dirt.

He put his bony arm around my shoulder. "Good on you, lassie. I knew this place wasn't meant for you all along. There's something better in life for a good hardworking girl like you. Go and find it. I'm sure you will."

He picked up his rake as if to get on with his job, but he still had something more to say.

"I'll be dead long gone when you grow up and have your little ones. Promise you'll be a good mother to them."

My tears splashed down on the leaves and dust as I whispered to Bill, "I will." Then he patted me on the back. "Good luck, girl," he said, and hobbled away. I forgot about asking him up for tea and cake. He left the Bigelows' shortly after, and I never saw Bill again.

Christmas

After having polished, cleaned up, and raked the gardens for a week solid, I was nearly dead on my feet when me and my mate were both dropped off in town early Christmas morning. We were told we could stay in town all day, as Christmas was a time for families—theirs, that is—and we would only be in the way.

They would pick us up late in the evening to clean up after their families had gone home.

We were glad to be together again, but both of us were feeling the hurt and pain, as this was the first Christmas we had spent alone. We both cried a bit, longing for the love and warmth we had experienced back in the mission. With no presents and no food, we felt all alone.

The streets were empty, though far away in the background we could hear kids screaming and laughing. Then all of a sudden we both got the same idea. We'd walk up the hill and see if there were any nuns in town. If there was anyone who would have compassion, it would surely have to be the nuns. We remembered from our times in town that we had seen kids from the convent on the hill.

Our walk up there was a bit quiet. It was only when we were coming close to the convent that we began discussing who would be the speaker to explain our situation. We were both frightened that we would get into trouble if the people who employed us found out. But we both took our chances, as we were feeling quite hungry by then—it was near to twelve o'clock.

Horsey said that I should do the talking because she might break down and cry. When we got to the door, I felt very brave. I had everything laid out in my mind as to what I wanted to say.

As the nun opened the door, I just about fell through the doorway. I broke down and cried, and my mate ended up having to speak up for us.

After hearing the story of our plight, the nun held her hands out to us and said, "Come in, children!" We were nervous as she told us to follow her down the corridor and into the chapel.

We knelt down with the nun and said a prayer. When we were finished, she told us to follow her into the dining room, where three other nuns were sitting. The scene reminded us of home and for the first time we felt Christmas in our hearts.

They had a beautiful Christmas tree with the most effective decorations. The little lights were all the colours of a rainbow, and there were bright-coloured tinsels everywhere. The nun who had welcomed us in—I guess she must have been the Mother Superior—introduced us to the other three and explained our situation; then they all got up and left the room.

When they came back in, they had a present each for me and my mate. They served a wonderful Christmas dinner with all the trimmings. We had never felt so happy since we left the mission.

After dinner we said prayers and joined in singing "Silent Night" with the nuns. Then Mother Superior told us that she had rung a dear friend of hers who owned a farm and that she was coming to pick us up. We could spend the rest of the afternoon down on the farm with this lady and her husband.

It didn't take very long for the people to come and get us. They were in their mid fifties and very pleasant. Both were plump in body with very white hair; the gentleman had a huge red nose and a belly to go with it. He was very short for his build; he reminded me of one of the seven dwarfs—Happy. And when me and my mate glanced at each other, we found it very hard not to laugh. His wife was very much like him in looks and height.

After Mother Superior introduced us, the lady took our bags, which were laden with our presents and goodies, and put them in the car. We climbed into the backseat and went off to a most enjoyable day.

Before Anne and I went back to our farms, I

told her how I felt about those people I worked for. I told her that I had started to hate the place and had made my mind up to leave, as I was sick and tired of their attitude towards me.

I just couldn't keep on working for her after meeting people like the nuns and their friends and dear old Bill, who I was going to miss a lot. I felt in myself that I could not continue on anymore, no matter what the circumstances were.

My mate knew the way I felt, and when the people arrived to pick us up, we knew in our hearts that although our good-byes weren't forever, perhaps we wouldn't be meeting at this old school bus stop ever again.

A'Wandering

One day I was in the kitchen doing a cleaning job when I came across a letter which was lying on the kitchen bench. It was addressed to me!

Very rarely did I receive any letters from home. Once I got one from the head priest, and it was left on the bench. So I presume she left this one for me the same way.

I picked it up, feeling very excited, wondering who could be writing to me. I just about tore the letter opening it up and read through it quickly. It was from my mate Kaylene, in Dunsborough. I gave out a sigh of relief. I knew it meant I would be leaving this unhappy place.

She wrote that I could come anytime. There was a weekly bus from Ridgeway travelling south to Busselton. Kaylene said she would drive in from Dunsborough to meet it every Friday, in case I would be on it. I couldn't tell Mrs. Bigelow about this. I put the letter away safely in my room and went on with my jobs.

A few weeks passed and I still couldn't get away. I was worrying about Kaylene going off to Busselton to meet the bus and me not being on it! But I had to wait for my normal holidays, when I could leave the farm and not be expected back for a couple of weeks. About late summer the time finally came for me to return to the mission to pay them a visit.

In her usual manner Mrs. Bigelow dropped me off at the bus station and left me to get my own ticket. There were two buses, one to Bunbury and one to Busselton. I went on board the bus to Bunbury, which would connect with the train to Armadale and so take me back to Wandering Mission. I sat there looking out the window.

I waited for her car to disappear. Then I jumped up from my seat, went down the aisle, collected my case, and changed buses. I then bought my ticket—to Busselton. I was very nervous and confused and felt frightened, as I didn't think I had the nerve to do it. Deep down inside me I was happy—a lot. I felt a heavy load lift off my shoulders as the bus I was on pulled out.

So when it was time for me to return to the mission, I never turned up. I went the other way! I was hoping Kaylene would be there at the stop in Busselton.

She welcomed me with open arms. I cried uncontrollably for a couple of minutes while she kept reassuring me that I was safe and she would look after me. I dried my eyes and felt a lot better, while Kaylene gathered my bags and case.

Before she drove me to her home in Dunsborough, she took me downtown into Busselton for a cup of tea and something to eat. On our way she told me how many kids she had, all about herself and her husband's work.

She asked me about the farm and the people. I poured everything out to her. Kaylene told me not to worry; she would see I got my own job, but not under those circumstances I'd left behind.

After a week of swimming and relaxing in my other world, I found I was a human being again. Then a letter came. Father wrote to Kaylene from the mission. Somehow he'd found out where I'd got to, as he was worried why I didn't turn up at the Armadale station.

I felt a little sad, and worried as to what would happen to me. "I don't want to go back to the mission," I told Kaylene. "I'll only end up on the farm again." Kaylene said she was in the bad books with the head priest too, as she encouraged me to come down to her and never let him know I was with her. She reassured me—she'd explain everything to Father when he came, in two days' time.

So we prepared for the visit. When he arrived, Kaylene stepped outside to greet him. I was back in the kitchen, making a cup of tea, as they came in the front door.

Kaylene sang out to me, "Come and say hello to Father!" I went through to the lounge nervously and saw Father holding out his hand. I trembled as I shook it, and murmured, "Hello,

Father . . .'' Kaylene said she'd leave us alone, as Father wanted to sort things out with me.

As Father went on to tell me that it was not good for a young girl like me to be out of work too long, I felt uneasy. He said that if I didn't find a job in three weeks' time, he was coming to get me and take me back to the mission. I could work there till he found me a proper position. My heart sank. I dreaded the thought of working on another farm.

Kaylene knocked on the door and came in with the tea and sandwiches. I started to relax and join in the conversation. After spending the day with us, he left, saying he would keep in touch. Kaylene was to let him know if I did get a job. So we said good-bye to Father.

The following week Kaylene drove me into Busselton Hospital to try to get an interview. I was feeling nervous, and she took me by the hand. The smell of Dettol hit us straightaway. We asked a nurse, ''Which way to the office?'' She told us to follow her down the long corridor. We passed a few wards. Then we were at the office.

Kaylene knocked again, and a firm voice answered inside, ''Come in!'' I followed her to where this sophisticated man was sitting behind his desk. He looked up at us, smiled, and we smiled back. ''What can I do for you?'' Kaylene introduced both of us and explained the situation, how I was wanting a job.

He said he couldn't help me for the time being, as he had about fifty women on his waiting list, but he could take my name and if anything came up, he would let me know. So we thanked his pleasant gentleman with a plump round face and left, feeling dispirited.

Two weeks after the job interview, I was getting desperate. It was a Sunday, and we were having dinner. There was knocking at the door. I went to open it, wondering who it was—could this be Father, coming for me?

I opened the door, and to my surprise it was the man from the hospital. He told me to pack my bags and throw them in the hospital ute. He had put me in front of all those ladies! He had even paid two weeks' rent for me in a boardinghouse in the town, and I could pay him back when I got to know a few people and could find a place of my own.

We were thrilled, me and Kaylene—I was a little bit sad to leave her, but she said not to worry. "I'll come and pick you up for days off." So I said good-bye to Dunsborough for the present, and we drove off.

There was no looking back for me.

Epilogue

I am happily married now,
To a very fine gentleman.
His name is Charlie,
A hairdresser by trade,
Who had the honour of being
The Governor's hairdresser.
We are blessed with two beautiful
Children, a girl we named
Jodi Anne, who is ten years old,
And a boy we named
Brian Ocean, who is eight years old.
I named him after my dead brother,
Who I had only seen
Once in my life.
There'll be no washing other
People's dishes, or
Getting dropped off at bus stops,
For any of my children.
We will be making sure that our
Kids will be given every opportunity
In their lives to get a good education,
So that they can take their places

In today's society as lawyers or doctors,
Or etc.—and be equal in the one human
Race!

About the Author

GLENYSE WARD, an Australian Aboriginal, was born in Perth and now lives with her husband and two children in Broome, Western Australia.